Speed Up Your Arabic

Pronunciation, spelling, the concept of roots and patterns, sentence structure, numbers and idiomatic phrases are just some of the areas that cause confusion for students of Arabic. Learning how to avoid the common errors that arise repeatedly in these areas is an essential step in successful language learning.

Speed Up Your Arabic is a unique and innovative resource that identifies and explains the most commonly made errors, enabling students to learn from their mistakes and enhance their understanding of the Arabic language.

Each of the nine chapters focuses on a grammatical category where English speakers typically make mistakes in Arabic. Each chapter is divided into sections that classify the concepts and errors into subcategories. Full explanations are provided throughout with clear, comprehensive examples and exercises to help the learner gain an in-depth understanding of Arabic grammar and usage.

Key features:

- carefully selected grammar topics and examples based on the most commonly made errors
- comprehensive explanations of the most difficult grammar points help learners gain an in-depth understanding of Arabic grammar and usage
- exercises throughout reinforce learning and link theory to practice
- a complete answer key, making it ideal for self-study
- a glossary of grammatical terms, an Arabic–English glossary and a bibliography to aid learning
- useful drills and listening samples available for free download at http://www.routledge.com/books/details/9780415660556/

Suitable both for classroom use and self-study, *Speed Up Your Arabic* is the ideal resource for all intermediate learners of Arabic wishing to refine their language skills.

Sebastian Maisel is Associate Professor for Arabic and Middle East Studies at Grand Valley State University, USA.

SPEED UP YOUR LANGUAGE SKILLS

SERIES EDITOR: Javier Muñoz-Basols, *University of Oxford, UK*

The *Speed Up Your Language Skills* series publishes innovative, high quality textbooks focusing on common errors as an effective tool to improve one's skills in a foreign language. Such errors are often either driven by linguistic transfer from English or caused by common misperceptions about the grammatical structure of a foreign language.

The primary objectives of the series are to explain and illustrate in context the most common errors made by English-speaking students in a foreign language and to classify them in easy-to-reference categories. Students can thus learn the appropriate usage of words and expressions and understand the reasons why they persistently make the same mistakes. The inclusion of exercises, shortcuts, mnemonic devices and much-needed strategies, not usually seen in conventional grammar books, facilitates vocabulary acquisition and mastery of essential grammatical elements.

Books in the series are intended as primary or supplementary texts at the intermediate and advanced levels. Due to its self-explanatory approach and user-friendly format, the series is also recommended for self-learners who wish to "speed up" their language skills.

Available titles in the series:

Speed Up Your Chinese
Shin Yong Robson

Speed Up Your Spanish
Javier Muñoz-Basols, Marianne David and Olga Núñez Piñeiro

Speed Up Your Arabic

Strategies to avoid common errors

تعلّم اللغة العربية

الأساليب الصحيحة في تفادي الأخطاء القبيحة

Sebastian Maisel

LONDON AND NEW YORK

First published 2015
by Routledge
2 Park Square, Milton Park, Abingdon, Oxon OX14 4RN

and by Routledge
711 Third Avenue, New York, NY 10017

Routledge is an imprint of the Taylor & Francis Group, an informa business

© 2015 Sebastian Maisel

The right of Sebastian Maisel to be identified as author of this work has been asserted by him in accordance with sections 77 and 78 of the Copyright, Designs and Patents Act 1988.

All rights reserved. No part of this book may be reprinted or reproduced or utilized in any form or by any electronic, mechanical, or other means, now known or hereafter invented, including photocopying and recording, or in any information storage or retrieval system, without permission in writing from the publishers.

Trademark notice: Product or corporate names may be trademarks or registered trademarks, and are used only for identification and explanation without intent to infringe.

British Library Cataloguing in Publication Data
A catalogue record for this book is available from the British Library

Library of Congress Cataloging in Publication Data
A catalog record for this book has been requested

ISBN: 978-0-415-66053-2 (hbk)
ISBN: 978-0-415-66055-6 (pbk)
ISBN: 978-1-315-73131-5 (ebk)

Typeset in Swiss and Zapf Calligraphic
by Graphicraft Limited, Hong Kong

Printed and bound in the United States of America by
Edwards Brothers Malloy on sustainably sourced paper

To my girls: Shannon, Fiona, Sophia and Cornelia

Contents

	Introduction	viii
1	**Pronunciation** النطق	1
2	**Spelling** الكتابة	13
3	**Roots and patterns** الجذر والوزن	29
4	**Nouns and adjectives** الاسم والصفة	39
5	**Speaking Arabic properly** الإعراب	66
6	**Verbs** الأفعال	77
7	**Word order and sentence structure** تركيب الجمل	95
8	**Numbers** الأرقام والأعداد	112
9	**Phrases, idioms and other key words** الأقوال والأمثال، العبارات والمصطلحات	126
	Answer key to exercises	142
	Arabic–English glossary قاموس عربي — انجليزي	183
	Bibliography	210
	Index and glossary of grammatical terms	211

Introduction

Speed Up Your Arabic is designed to help non-native students of Arabic to reach a higher level of proficiency, at the same time refining their critical language skills. The major aspects of Arabic syntax and morphology are illuminated, highlighting areas problematic for lower-level students, especially common errors. Not surprisingly, students of all levels commit similar mistakes when trying to understand the basic structures and functions of Arabic words, phrases and sentences. Based on my experience of teaching Arabic to different levels, I have found that students carry with them common errors picked up at the beginner and early intermediate stages, mostly in the areas of pronunciation, spelling, and word and sentence structure. Although nowadays an immense pool of language material is available online, and there are textbooks for each level, I have found that no resource specifically addresses these common mistakes. Little or no help is available to reinforce fundamental grammatical concepts and vocabulary practice.

Highlighting these false conceptions and concurrently offering practical solutions and training to avoid such errors are the main objectives of this book. These common errors are too often ignored, which is why they are persistently made. This book is intended to be used as a practical supplement in the classroom or for self-study.

The book is structured to gradually expose the student to fundamental concepts of Arabic, starting with the correct pronunciation and spelling of the Arabic alphabet. This is followed by an introduction to the core aspects of Arabic syntax and morphology and culminates with original native idioms, key words and phrases. Each chapter provides examples of correct usage as well as common mistakes made by non-native learners, which helps to refine the main grammatical message. Additional notes, tips and mnemonic devices are included to highlight the learning outcome: recognizing and correcting common errors.

Each section of the book uses examples of correct and incorrect usage to illustrate the issue. These examples come directly from the classroom and represent the most common errors language learners repeatedly commit. After these errors have been identified and explained the book provides strategies and exercises to avoid them in the future. If appropriate, comparisons with English grammar are made. Making these associations allows the student to better understand the general linguistic concepts which both Arabic and English are built upon. Data was collected over a period of several years in Arabic language classes for elementary and intermediate levels at universities in the USA and Germany.

Chapter 1 deals with issues of (not) properly pronouncing Arabic sounds. Saying something wrong in a foreign language is not a terrible thing, but pronouncing something wrongly can lead to embarrassing moments. Too often a thick accent is kept for ever. Arabic has a few unique sounds with no equivalents in the English alphabet. Also, two Arabic words may only differ in one tiny short vowel, which makes proper pronunciation even more important. This chapter contains solutions to the problem of how to sound like a native speaker and to avoid English slang in Arabic.

Chapter 2 reviews the Arabic alphabet and looks at common errors in spelling and writing. Although computerized text production is becoming more frequent, there are still many situations in daily life when a spell checker is not available. This chapter reviews all aspects of writing and spelling, such as the alphabet, silent letters and hamza, and enables students to improve their writing skills.

Chapter 3 reviews the most important tool for learning Arabic, the concept of root and pattern. Comprehending this system is like a life vest for you: even if you don't know or remember the word you are trying to say, you can create it on the spot. You may want to argue about the way the tool is taught, but after learning it correctly, you will appreciate it greatly.

Chapter 4 looks at the largest group of words: nouns and adjectives, and focuses on avoiding agreement errors. The importance of gender, number, state and case is stressed, which are often different from English grammar. Students repeatedly begin by relying on their native syntax, often translating literally and word-by-word into the target language. The segments of the iDaafa are often switched and the wrong word is marked with the article. Generally, the wrong use of the definite article is a major error. But in Arabic it all starts with a simple noun–adjective phrase that can be extended by adding attributes, verbs, prefixes and even completed sentences. And all of these pieces need to agree with the main noun of the sentence or phrase.

Chapter 5 covers the case endings, or declension of Arabic nouns and adjectives, which is considered the biggest challenge for native and non-native speakers. Using the case endings, or the i'raab, however, means to speak Arabic properly. Although some believe that the i'raab is not for the intermediate level, in this chapter students will learn how important it can be and how to master it. With a little help from English grammar and simple linguistics,

x *Introduction*

students will quickly realize that i'raab can be fun. And it is an easy way to impress native speakers.

Chapter 6 covers various aspects of the Arabic verb. Although Arabic recognizes the concept of sentences without verbs, intimate familiarity with verb conjugations in different tenses and modes is a sign of higher proficiency. While the sheer challenge of using verbs frequently is already difficult for non-native speakers, they also have to internalize original Arabic concepts about verbs in order to avoid sounding like a non-native speaker. The absence of an Arabic equivalent of the verb "to be" is another hurdle for beginners. How to use verbs properly and with confidence is thus the main theme of this chapter.

Chapter 7 clarifies another difficult area for students of Arabic: word order and sentence structure. Grammatically, this is the most distant field when comparing English and Arabic syntax. Producing longer sentences and sentences of different types, such as relative or conditional sentences, indicates a higher level of proficiency. In order to reach this level, students must give up English grammatical concepts and actively use unfamiliar structures. It is obvious that lower-level students struggle with this and often confuse the various sentence types and word orders. This chapter helps to set the record straight and put the sentence structure right.

Chapter 8 deals only with numbers. Simple understanding and even memorizing of some Arabic numbers is a small step; however, the correct use of cardinal and ordinal numbers becomes a serious undertaking which many students struggle with. On the other hand, it is crucial to know your numbers when doing banking, finance, selling, buying or measuring things. Unfortunately, students regularly mix the two varieties of numbers and confuse important agreement rules, thus the need to include this special review of numbers.

Chapter 9 looks at key words, idiomatic expressions and other important connectors, particles and phrases. The field of Arabic semantics and vocabulary is very large. Communication, both oral and written, includes many stereotypical phrases and ready-to-use expressions. Because Arabic has only very few cognates, the issue of false friends deserves less attention than the proper knowledge and use of key words, sayings, proverbs and other particles. In fact, false friends are very rare; they only occur through loan translations, usually from English.

However, it is advisable to practice these concepts with native speakers, instructors, tutors, friends and peers. Soon enough you will find that they commit mistakes too, because nobody is perfect:

جلّ مَن لا يُخْطِئ

An answer key to the exercises can be found at the end of the book. Several online drills and listening samples are available for free download at http://www.routledge.com/books/details/9780415660556/.

1 Pronunciation
النطق

1 The letters	2
1.1 Equivalent letters	2
1.2 Original Arabic letters	3
1.3 Vowels	5
2 Diphthongs	5
3 Emphatic letters الحروف المفخمة	6
4 Sun and moon letters	7
5 Hamza	9
6 Stress	10
7 Taa marbuuTa ة **in the** إضافة	11

2 *Speed Up Your Arabic*

The correct pronunciation of Arabic sounds and letters is a hurdle for many novice learners of Arabic. If not taught properly at the beginner's stage, mis-pronunciations carry on to the next level. Repetitive practice with the instructor, peers, Arab friends and relatives is essential. In addition, students should familiarize themselves with Arabic sounds by listening to radio programs, watching films, and interacting with native speakers.

1 The letters

The Arabic alphabet includes 34 phonemes: 28 consonants, three long vowels and three short vowels in addition to two diphthongs. Their correct pronunciation can be achieved easily, because with the exception of three letters, all of the sounds are also found in the English alphabet.

1.1 Equivalent letters

س	ز	ر	ذ	د	ج	ث	ت	ب	أ
siin	zay	raa	dhaal	daal	jiim	thaa	taa	baa	alif
s	z	r	dh	d	j	th	t	b	a

و	ي	ه	ن	م	ل	ك	ف	ش
waw	yaa	haa	nuun	miim	laam	kaaf	faa	shiin
w	y	h	n	m	l	k	f	sh

Emphatic letters

ص	ض	ط	ظ
Saad	Daad	Taa	Dhaa
S	D	T	Dh

These four letters are called emphatic letters and their pronunciation is the same as their corresponding English letters; however, the difference is in the pronunciation of the surrounding vowels, which become darker and more hollow.

Examples:

ص – س

	Saad ص	siin س
Arabic letter		
Arabic sound example	صار	سار
Transliteration	Saar	saar
English sound example	saw	sad

3 Pronunciation النطق

د - ض

Arabic letter	Daad ض	daal د
Arabic sound example	ضباب	دباب
Transliteration	Dabaab	dabbaab
English sound example	dark	dad

ت - ط

Arabic letter	Taa ط	taa ت
Arabic sound example	طابع	تابع
Transliteration	Taabi'	taabi'
English sound example	tall	tame

ذ - ظ

Arabic letter	Dhaa ظ	dhaal ذ
Arabic sound example	ظليل	ذليل
Transliteration	Dhaliil	dhaliil
English sound example	those	that

1.2 Original Arabic letters

Of the five remaining letters, two are uncommon in English, while three are unique to Arabic.

The letter khaa (خ) is a deep, coarse sound from your throat equal to the Scottish word Loch or the German composer Bach. The letter ghayn (غ) is another "r"-sound, but unlike the raa (ر) that is produced by rolling your tongue, this one is made down in your throat. The sound is often compared to that of gargling. Try this for a while with water and focus on the muscles you use. The sound of ghayn is very close to the French "r" such as in rue or frère.

The three letters that have no English equivalent are:

ق	ع	ح
qaaf	ayn	Haa
q	'	H

> **Tip: How do you properly pronounce these letters?**
> The letter Haa or ح is arguably the easiest of the three. Exhale strongly. Make an effort and breathe out some air. Imagine yourself checking your breath when you exhale. Or for those of you who wear glasses and need to clean them quickly: don't you breathe some air onto them? The same effort is needed to pronounce Haa.

4 *Speed Up Your Arabic*

The letter ayn, or ع, is considered by many to be the hardest letter to pronounce. But unfortunately, it is also a very frequent letter. So, get your throat muscles engaged, press hard to get the air out (through your throat!), open your mouth wide and squeeze out a sound that includes a vowel. Ayn, like hamza, is best pronounced in combination with a vowel. I have also heard another tip: imagine yourself singing a very deep note. Whatever works for you, don't forget to press and open wide.

The letter qaaf, or ق, is essentially just another "k" sound, only from much deeper in your throat. Try saying "kaaf" as low as you can with your mouth wide open. Engage the muscles in your throat! Don't be fooled by the transliteration of the letter with "q". Because the letter is so hard for many people, even Arabs, its pronunciation has changed in many Arabic dialects. In Egypt, Morocco and urban areas of the Levant it is often pronounced like a hamza as a glottal stop, while in rural areas of Jordan and Palestine and in many areas of the Arabian Peninsula it has become a "g" sound.

Examples:

Khaliiji (Gulf Arabic)	miSri (Egyptian)	MSA
dageega	da'ee'a	daqeeqa

Exercises

EXERCISE 1. Read the following words containing the Arabic letter ح. Check the correct pronunciation using the website.

صَحيح	يُحافِظ	حاج
نَجاح	مُحَمَّد	حُرية
نوح	مَحبوب	حَديث
مِلح	تَحتَ	حُروف
مِنَح	مَحَلّ	حتى

EXERCISE 2. Read the following words containing the Arabic letter ع. Check the correct pronunciation using the website.

شارِع	مَعنا	عام
فُروع	ساعة	عَدَد
واسِع	فِعل	العِراق
طَوابِع	أعْياد	عُمان
اِجتِماع	يَعمَل	عَوْدة

Pronunciation النطق 5

EXERCISE 3. Read the following words containing the Arabic letter ق. Check the correct pronunciation using the website.

دقائق	أقسام	القاهِرة
لَقلَق	أقارِب	قِسم
أحمق	يَقول	قُمامة
فُستُق	مُقابَلة	قرية
فَريق	تَقرير	قَمَر

1.3 Vowels

Modern Standard Arabic has three long vowel sounds, their short equivalents and two diphthongs.

The three long vowels are:

Arabic vowel	ي	و	ا
English pronunciation	ee as in "deer"	oo as in "root"	aa as in "bath"

The three short vowels are:

Written symbol	—	—	—
Short vowel name	كسرة/kasra	ضمة/Damma	فتحة/fatHa
Short vowel sound	i	u	a

Note that the Arabic vowel sounds are not identical to the English vowel sounds. Modern Standard Arabic has only three short and three long vowel sounds, and they are easy to articulate. In the various Arabic dialects additional vowel sounds can be found. Regarding the difference between short and long sounds, compare them to musical notes where you would hold a half note longer than a quarter note. Long vowels are like half notes and thus need to be held longer. This is important because some words can only be distinguished by the length of the vowel.

Examples:

the company car	sayaarat ash-sharika	سيارة الشركة
the company cars	sayaaraat ash-sharika	سيارات الشركة

2 Diphthongs

Diphthongs represent a vowel combination of fatHa – waw – sukuun وْ or fatHa – yaa – sukuun يْ . The English equivalent sound is in "powder" and "eye".

6 *Speed Up Your Arabic*

Examples:

English	Transliteration	Arabic	English	Transliteration	Arabic
night	layla	لَيْلة	sleep	nawm	نَوْم
house	bayt	بَيْت	unity	tawHiid	تَوْحيد
Faysal	FaySal	فَيْصَل	position	mawqi'	مَوْقِع

Exercise

EXERCISE 4. Listen to the words on the website and mark those that contain a diphthong.

Diphthong?	الكلمة	Diphthong?	الكلمة	Diphthong?	الكلمة
_____	ليس	_____	توحيد	_____	الكون
_____	اشتريت	_____	خير	_____	مشيت
_____	صحونا	_____	السيطرة	_____	السيرة
_____	الضمير	_____	موجود	_____	بيروت
_____	بحيرة	_____	عيون	_____	ثوم

3 Emphatic letters الحروف المفخمة

See also section 1.1 above.

The following sounds represent a special category of emphatic letters. Although literally the same as the non-emphatic sounds, in their correct pronunciation they affect the vowels surrounding them and make them sound darker. This distinction is very important.

Listening sample 1 (online)

Listen and compare the pronunciation of the emphatic and the non-emphatic letters.

Non-emphatic letter	Emphatic letter	Emphatic (non-emphatic) letter
سَيْف	صَيْف	ص (س)
دباب	ضُباب	ض (د)
تابع	طابع	ط (ت)
ذَليل	ظَليل	ظ (ذ)
كابوس	قابوس	ق (ك)

Pronunciation النطق 7

Exercise

EXERCISE 5. Listen to the exercise on the website and mark the words you hear.

قلب		كلب
كابوس		قابوس
مقر		مكان
صديقة		سكينة
تمر		طميم
مطلوب		متهم
دليل		ذلك
العُسر		اليُسر
هيئة		حيّة
مقصود		مكسور

4 Sun and moon letters

Arabic is a language in which almost every letter and sound is pronounced, unlike French or Polish, where several letters form a sound cluster. The exceptions to the rule are the sun and moon letters (الحروف الشمسية والقمرية). The differentiation between sun letters and moon letters is confusing at first and surprisingly often forgotten by students. Frequently, sun letters are not pronounced at all. In writing, sun letters are spelled wrong.

Listening sample 2 (online)

Listen to the correct pronunciation of the sun letters:

	خطأ		صواب
النطق	al-shajara al-Tawiila		ash-shajara aT-Tawiila
الكتابة	اشجرة اطويلة		الشجرة الطويلة

The regular sound of these letters is pronounced differently when following the definite article (ألـ). In the case of the sun letters, the laam ل of the article ألـ is omitted and the first letter of the word is lengthened or doubled by the shadda. With the moon letters, this rule does not apply. Here the article is fully articulated, followed by the first letter of the word.

The sun letters are: ن ل ظ ط ض ص ش س ز ر ذ د ث ت

The moon letters are: ي و هـ م ك ق ف غ ع خ ح ج ب ء

8 Speed Up Your Arabic

Tip

These letters are called sun and moon letters based on the two Arabic sample words "sun" (*shams* شمس) and "moon" (*qamar* قمر). The first letter of *shams* is ش and requires assimilation, while the first letter of *qamar*, ق, does not.

Mnemonic device

اِبْغِ حَجَّكَ وخَفْ عَميقَهُ

This otherwise meaningless sentence helps you to memorize the moon letters. It consists of the 14 moon letters only.

Listening sample 3 (online)

Listen to the correct pronunciation of the sun and moon letters.

		الحروف القمرية			الحروف الشمسية
the moon	al-qamar	القمر	the sun	ash-shams	الشَّمس
the fall	al-khariif	الخريف	the car	as-sayaara	السيارة
philosophy	al-falsafa	الفلسفة	the student	aT-Taalib	الطالب
dignity	al-karaama	الكرامة	the men	ar-rijaal	الرجال
the rose	al-warda	الوردة	the light	an-nuur	النور

Exercise

EXERCISE 6. Can you notice the difference between the sun and moon letters? Identify the words that start with a sun letter by writing ش and those starting with a moon letter by writing ق.

_____	الليل	_____	الصباح
_____	الرمال	_____	الكرسي
_____	الديموقراطية	_____	المتحف
_____	الضمير	_____	الديوان
_____	الرياض	_____	السماء
_____	التفاح	_____	الورقة

Pronunciation النطق 9

	الطائرة		الزبون
	الظلم		الاختبار
	العيون		الفنون
	السياسة		الذهاب

5 Hamza

The first letter of the alphabet is hamza, or a voiceless glottal stop. Very often, students do not recognize hamza as a real letter. They also frequently confuse the letter ayn with hamza. In order to articulate hamza it needs vowel sounds to create a syllable. If located at the beginning of a word, hamza always "sits" on the letter alif. In unvocalized text it is unclear which short vowel sound it represents (fatHa, Damma or kasra). This makes it seem as if all words start with the letter alif. But as a general rule, Arabic words do not start with a long vowel sound. Whenever you hear a vowel at the beginning of an Arabic word there is a hamza carrying the short vowel. You only have to write the alif with hamza.

For the rules of writing hamza, see Chapter 2.

Listening sample 4 (online)

Listen to these examples of hamza sounds.

ibn	إبن	udhn	أذن	anf	أنف
imaam	إمام	ukht	أُخت	adhhab	أذهب
imkaaniya	إمكانية	udkhul	أُدْخُل	alladhi	أَلَذي

Note that all of these words start with a short vowel sound. In writing, this sound is represented by the alif with hamza and a short vowel sound.

The "a" sound and the alif often cause confusion. And it gets a little bit more complicated. There are additional long "a" sounds besides the regular alif. Luckily, they are very rare and you can easily memorize the spelling of those few words. They include the alif madda, alif qaSiira (also called dagger alif) and the alif maqSuura, all representing a long "aa" vowel at different positions within a word.

Examples:

alif madda: آخر , الآن
alif qaSiira: هذا , الله , لكن
alif maqSuura: إلى , مشى , مصطفى

6 Stress

At the beginner's level, students are not accustomed to the stress of Arabic words. Frequently, the wrong syllable is stressed. However, unlike English, where stress is often unpredictable, Arabic offers guidelines that indicate the emphasis or stress in each word. A simple rule of thumb is to stress the syllable with the long vowel.

ki-**taab**
ma-**dii**-na
maa-lik

But many words don't have long vowels. In order to place the stress on the correct syllable, one should start counting the syllables from the end of a word, because stress can only go on the last three syllables of a word. The last syllable of a word is rarely pronounced, only if it includes a long vowel. But as mentioned before, the stress very often goes on the long vowel (if applicable). When adding إعراب endings or suffixes, i.e. adding additional syllables, the stress moves accordingly to the next syllable.

Listening sample 5 (online)

Listen to the correct word stress.

an-tum
ya-ta-dhak-ka-**ruu**-na-hum
ma-dra-sa
ma-**dra**-sa-tun
ku-tub
ku-**tu**-bu-naa

Exercise

EXERCISE 7. Write the number of the syllable that is stressed in the following Arabic words.

_____	مُستَقبَل	١	شَجَرة
_____	مُستَقبَلُهُم	_____	أصْحاب
_____	قِصَص	_____	مُساعَدة
_____	إقتِصاد	_____	يَزورونَه
_____	أحِبّ	_____	رَجُل

Pronunciation النطق 11

Tip
The best way of familiarizing yourself with Arabic pronunciation and correct stress is through watching Arabic television and listening to music and radio shows. Even if you don't understand a lot of what is discussed, you will get a feeling for the sound, pitch and stress. Having a native speaker as a conversation partner helps too; however, be aware that he or she might pronounce things differently in his or her native dialect.

7 Taa marbuuTa ة in the إضافة

Another rare case of not articulating the "real" sound of the letter is the taa marbuuTa ة. In most cases the taa marbuuTa ة marks the female gender and is pronounced like a short "a" except when used in the إضافة (see Chapter 4), when two nouns form a compound and it is pronounced "at". It then serves as a placeholder for the grammatical case ending or إعراب (see Chapter 5).

Listening sample 6 (online)

Listen to the examples.

Madina	مدينة
Madina**tun**	مدينةٌ
madina**t** Baghdad	مدينة بغداد
madina**tu** Baghdad	مدينةُ بغداد

Exercises

EXERCISE 8. Decide how to read the female ending of the first noun, whether to read "at" or "a".

	الجامعة الحكومية		المدينة الجميلة
_____	الأستاذة فاطمة	_____	الحكومة التونسية
_____	العلاقة السياسية	_____	حكومة دولة قطر
_____	العلاقة بين الدولتين	_____	سيارة والدي
_____	مدينة الرياض	_____	جامعة الدول العربية

EXERCISE 9. Listen to the tongue twisters on the website and practice reading them. Then memorize them.

لحم الحمام حلال ولحم الحمار حرام

خيط حرير على حيط خليل

خوخ الشيخ خوش خوخ

طير طار على جِدار دار طَهَ ... جِدار دار طَهَ جِدار طين

المشمش دة مش من مشمشكم ... مكان المشمش دة مش من مشمشنا

EXERCISE 10. English has adopted many words from Arabic. Read the Arabic word and match it with the English equivalent.

lute	السَفَر
sugar	أمير البحر
giraffe	العود
adobe	مَخزن
coffee	الزرافة
safari	قُطن
cotton	الجَرّ
assassin	قُماش دِمَشْقي
admiral	الكُحول
damask	قَهوة
algebra	الطوبة
magazine	الخوارزمي
alcohol	حَشيشين
jar	الجابر
algorithm	سُكر

2 Spelling
الكتابة

1 The alphabet الأبجدية	**14**
1.1 Handwritten Arabic versus typed Arabic	17
2 Writing hamza	**18**
2.1 Hamza at the beginning of a word	18
2.2 Hamza in the middle of a word	18
2.3 Hamza at the end of a word	19
3 Dots or no dots: that is the question	**19**
3.1 Taa marbuuTa ة versus haa ه	19
3.2 Alif maqSuura ى versus yaa ي	20
4 Misplaced dots	**20**
5 Connected and unconnected letters	**21**
6 Silent and invisible letters	**22**
6.1 Silent alif وا	22
6.2 تنوين of fatHa	23
6.3 Dagger alif	23
6.4 Taa marbuuTa ة in the إضافة	23
6.5 Sun and moon letters	23
6.6 Taa marbuuTa ة after alif	24
7 Writing numbers	**24**
7.1 Two and three	25
7.2 Numbering and listing items	25
8 Special cases and ligatures	**26**
9 Writing Arabic dialects	**27**

14 *Speed Up Your Arabic*

'HAMMAAM' = BATHROOM   and   'HAMAM' = PIGEON

ضِع النقاط على الحروف!
Put the dots on the letters!

Among the most common errors at the beginner's level in writing Arabic are the connectors between letters, the diacritical markers, the dots and the confusion over handwritten versus typed letters. Moving on to the intermediate level, it becomes difficult for students to recognize silent letters or those that are pronounced differently from their spelling. Also, the different spelling rules for Arabic dialects cause problems. At the end of the chapter we look at a new form of Arabic writing that uses Latin letters and numerals; it is called Arabizi.

1 The alphabet الأبجدية

Arabic is a cursive script written from right to left. Each letter has four different shapes depending on its position in the word. There is a distinct shape at the beginning, the middle and the end of the word as well as when the letter is written independently, i.e. not connected to the right or left. The letters have different sizes, but no capital letters exist.

Spelling الكتابة 15

Name of letter	Transliteration	Independent	Final	Medial	Initial
hamza	'	ء	ئ، ؤ، أ، إ	ئ، ؤ، أ	أ، إ، ئـ، ؤ، أ
alif	aa	ا	ـا	ـا	ا
baa	b	ب	ـب	ـبـ	بـ
taa	t	ت	ـت	ـتـ	تـ
thaa	th	ث	ـث	ـثـ	ثـ
jiim	j	ج	ـج	ـجـ	جـ
Haa	H	ح	ـح	ـحـ	حـ
khaa	kh	خ	ـخ	ـخـ	خـ
daal	d	د	ـد	ـد	د
dhal	dh	ذ	ـذ	ـذ	ذ
raa	r	ر	ـر	ـر	ر
zay	z	ز	ـز	ـز	ز
siin	s	س	ـس	ـسـ	سـ
shiin	sh	ش	ـش	ـشـ	شـ
Saad	S	ص	ـص	ـصـ	صـ
Daad	D	ض	ـض	ـضـ	ضـ
Taa	T	ط	ـط	ـطـ	ط
Dhaa	DH	ظ	ـظ	ـظـ	ظ
ayn	'	ع	ـع	ـعـ	عـ
ghayn	gh	غ	ـغ	ـغـ	غـ
faa	f	ف	ـف	ـفـ	فـ
qaaf	q	ق	ـق	ـقـ	قـ
kaaf	k	ك	ـك	ـكـ	كـ
laam	l	ل	ـل	ـلـ	لـ
miim	m	م	ـم	ـمـ	مـ
nuun	n	ن	ـن	ـنـ	نـ
haa	h	ه	ـه	ـهـ	هـ
waw	w, uu	و	ـو	ـو	و
yaa	y, ii	ي	ـي	ـيـ	يـ

Note that Arabic writing cannot do "printed" letters. As shown in the chart above it is essential to connect or not connect individual letters. That is why it is difficult to do crossword puzzles in Arabic. Seeing the independent shapes of the letters connected looks weird and incorrect, but try it yourself:

16 *Speed Up Your Arabic*

Exercises

EXERCISE 1. Can you find the ten words hidden in the grid below? All the words are related to seasons and weather. Remember the article.

ي	ا	ل	م	ط	ر	و	ل	ا
م	ل	و	م	ه	م	ر	ن	ي
ء	ز	ه	و	س	ا	ف	ء	س
ا	ه	ل	ي	ا	ل	ص	ي	ف
ت	و	ا	غ	ح	ب	ش	ل	ي
ش	ر	ح	ل	ا	ر	ب	ا	ر
ل	و	ب	ا	ب	د	و	ر	خ
ا	ي	ا	ل	ش	م	س	ي	ل
ق	ن	ز	ع	ي	ب	ر	ل	ا

EXERCISE 2. Listen to the words on the website and write them down. Check the correct spelling in the answer key.

Part 1

١	٢	٣	٤
_____	_____	_____	_____
٥	٦	٧	٨
_____	_____	_____	_____
٩	١٠	١١	١٢
_____	_____	_____	_____
١٣	١٤	١٥	١٦
_____	_____	_____	_____
١٧	١٨	١٩	٢٠
_____	_____	_____	_____

Part 2

٢١	٢٢	٢٣	٢٤
_____	_____	_____	_____
٢٥	٢٦	٢٧	٢٨
_____	_____	_____	_____
٢٩	٣٠	٣١	٣٢
_____	_____	_____	_____
٣٣	٣٤	٣٥	٣٦
_____	_____	_____	_____
٣٧	٣٨	٣٩	٤٠
_____	_____	_____	_____

Spelling الكتابة 17

In Chapter 1 we heard about the three short vowels and other markers (diacritics). Please remember that they are not written except in religious texts and some children's books, and only the long vowels and the diphthongs are actually written as full letters. It is helpful to simply imagine how an English text would look when written without vowels. You can still figure out the meaning of the sentence:

Wlcm t rbc clss!

These markers include the short vowels فَتْحَة – fatHa (short a), ضَمّة – Damma (short u) and كَسْرة – kasra (short i) as well as the سُكون – sukuun (indicates the absence of a vowel sound) and the شَدّة – shadda (a sign for doubling of the letter).

1.1 Handwritten Arabic versus typed Arabic

I recommend that you work on your handwriting skills; however, I also recognize that we write less and less by hand and use keyboards on computers, iPads, and cellphones more often. Check the positions of the Arabic letters on the PC and Apple keyboards. They differ slightly!

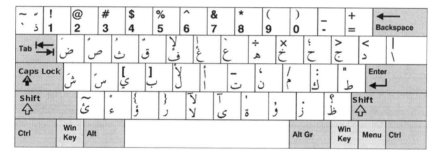

Layout of Arabic keyboard for Windows

Layout of Arabic keyboard for Apple/MAC

18 *Speed Up Your Arabic*

2 Writing hamza

Writing the letter hamza is arguably the most difficult writing task. Students at elementary and intermediate levels, even at advanced level, regularly misspell words that contain hamza. Since it occurs at different positions in a word – the beginning, the middle and/or the end – it requires special training to recognize the correct form. Beginners are recommended to practice writing those few familiar words that contain hamza.

Examples:

خطأ	صواب	خطأ	صواب
الريس	الرئيس	مع أصدقاي	مع أصدقائي
شوأن	شؤون	قرَتُ	قرأتُ
يرسال	إرسال	الزملة	الزملاء

When writing hamza it is important to determine on which letter (أ, ؤ or ئ) hamza sits or if it is written directly on the line. The carrying letter is called the "chair" (كرسي) and is determined by the vowels surrounding the hamza. Subsequently, one would find hamza at the beginning, in the middle or at the final position of a word. At the beginning of a word, hamza always sits on a chair, the letter alif.

2.1 Hamza at the beginning of a word

Arabic words never start with a long vowel; however, short vowels are very common. They are connected to the letters alif and hamza. Thus, whenever you hear an Arabic word starting with a vowel sound, you have to write alif as the first letter regardless of whether the sound is kasra or Damma.

Examples:

إسْنَان   أُذْن   أَنْف

2.2 Hamza in the middle of a word

This is arguably the most difficult case. This book targets the intermediate level, and the rules of writing hamza in the middle of a word are too complex for that level of proficiency. Therefore I will refer you to a thorough explanation of the topic in Schulz/Maisel.[1]

However, for the purpose of this book it is important to know that the hamza chair is determined by the surrounding vowels. Therefore I recommend listening carefully

---

1 Eckehard Schulz with Sebastian Maisel: *Al-Arabiya al-Mu'asira – Modern Standard Arabic: Textbook Integrating Main Arabic Dialects.* Edition Hamouda, Leipzig, 2013.

to the short and long vowel sounds as well as the distinct glottal stop. It also helps to memorize the spelling of the most common words with hamza in the middle.

Examples:

يَسْأَل   أسئلة   سؤال
قراءة   رئيس   مسؤول

2.3 Hamza at the end of a word

If hamza is preceded by a short vowel, then the equivalent long vowel will be the chair. If it is preceded by a long vowel or sukuun, it will sit by itself.

شَيْء   لؤلؤ   أصْدِقَاء

Exercise

EXERCISE 3. Write the word in Arabic with hamza in the correct form. You can listen to the words on the website.

ism (name)	_____	ukht (sister)	_____
akhbaar (news)	_____	ibn (son)	_____
ustaadh (professor)	_____	abwaab (doors)	_____
bi'r (well)	_____	qiraa'a (reading)	_____
ra'at (she saw)	_____	ra'iis (president)	_____
mas'uul (responsible)	_____	muruu'a (manliness)	_____
masaa' (evening)	_____	mabda' (principle)	_____
lu'lu' (pearl)	_____	su' (ill)	_____
shaaTi' (beach)	_____	zumalaa' (colleagues)	_____

3 Dots or no dots: that is the question

3.1 Taa marbuuTa ة versus haa ه

Many Arabic writers (and students) do not write the dots over the taa marbuuTa ة, making it look like a final haa ه. This can lead to misinterpretations and often confuses students who are unfamiliar with that habit; however, it is more likely that a word ends on a taa marbuuTa ة.

خطأ   صواب

مدينه   مدينة
في المدينه   في المدينة

The final haa ه is a common possessive pronoun and as such does not follow words with a definite article.

Examples:

| in his city | في مدينته |
| in the city | في المدينة |

3.2 Alif maqSuura ى versus yaa ي

Remember that alif maqSuura ى only occurs at the end of a word. Both letters have the same body, but only the yaa ي has two dots below. Some writers tend to omit the dots of the yaa ي, which can be confusing. However, remember that only a few words end with alif maqSuura ى, while the final yaa ي is a common possessive pronoun or nisba ending.

Examples:

| prayer hall | المصلى |
| worshiper, the one who prays | المصلي |

Exercise

EXERCISE 4. Correct the following sentences by deciding which letter is needed, taa marbuuTa ة or haa ه, and alif maqSuura ى or yaa ي?

أتمنى لك الصحه والعافيه. _____

في بيته غرف كثيره. _____

مدينته جميله. _____

المنبه تحت الوساده. _____

جاء أصحابي الى. _____

في المقهى كراسى فارغه. _____

4 Misplaced dots

As you can imagine, missing dots or putting them in the wrong place can lead to major misunderstandings. This often occurs in handwriting and requires taking a closer look at the words in order to identify the correct spelling.

It is also very common in Arabic handwriting to replace two or three dots by a line or a hook.

Spelling الكتابة 21

Examples:

Exercise

EXERCISES 5. Re-write the following handwritten text and pay close attention to the dots.

5 Connected and unconnected letters

Specific rules dictate which Arabic letter connects to the next or previous one and which does not.

Mnemonic device
Some Arabic letters (أ , د , ذ , ر , ز , و) do not connect to the left. Imagine a group of children holding hands left and right. These are your Arabic letters connecting on the left and right to the previous or following letter. However, some children do not follow the rules and let go of one hand. These kids include داوود and ذرة and زارا. Naughty little letters they are!

Exercise

EXERCISE 6. Form words by connecting the following letters.

_____	ش + ج + ر + ة	_____	ب + ا + ب
_____	ل + ذ + ي + ذ	_____	ح + ب + ي + ب
_____	و + ر + ق	_____	ح + ق + و + ق
_____	م + م + ل	_____	ج + د + ي + د
_____	ه + ذ + ه	_____	ت + م + ر
_____	د + ع + و + ة	_____	ك + ل + ا + م
_____	ش + ج + ا + ع	_____	أ + ل + ل + ه
_____	أ + ش + ي + ا + ء	_____	ر + ئ + ي + س
_____	ل + أ + ن + ه	_____	ذ + و + ي
_____	ظ + ن + و + ا	_____	ر + ا + د + ي + و

6 Silent and invisible letters

Generally, Arabic is a simple phonetic language, aside from the fact that you cannot read it immediately due to the missing short vowels. But you soon find out that you can read what is written right away with a few notable exceptions. Students always forget to write them, but grammar teachers love those silent letters which must be written, but are not pronounced. Luckily Arabic has only a few of these.

6.1 Silent alif وا

The هم form of verbs in the past carries a silent alif. It also appears in the plural form of verbs in the منصوب and مجزوم (see Chapter 6, section 7). However, remember that the silent alif will be dropped when an object pronoun is added to the verb.

Examples:

They want to go out in the afternoon.	يريدون أن يخرجوا بعد الظهر.
They did not finish their homework.	لم ينجزوا واجباتهم.
They wanted to help her.	أرادوا أن يساعدوها.

Spelling الكتابة 23

6.2 تنوين of fatHa

We have already learnt that Arabic words do not start with a long alif. Neither do they usually end on one. However, you will find some words with the alif in the final position. This is either the dual marker or the case marker for masculine adverbs, indefinite singular masculine nouns and broken plurals (see Chapter 5, section 4). Because the latter is considered a grammatical case ending of the إِعْراب it is rarely pronounced. But you still have to write it!

6.3 Dagger alif

Here is a long vowel, the "aa" sound, which is not written. Luckily, this old spelling convention occurs in only a few, although important, words.

Examples:

لكن	هذه	هذا	ألله
laakin	haadhihi	haadhaa	Allaah

6.4 Taa marbuuTa ة in the إِضافة

If the first word in the إِضافة is a female noun ending in a taa marbuuTa ة, this letter is often pronounced "at" instead of the regular "a" sound. Students commonly forget to say this extra letter/syllable. Also, during dictations you must remember not to write taa ت, but taa marbuuTa ة instead.

Listening sample 7 (online)

You can listen to the examples below on the website.

sayyaarat waalidii	سيارة والدي
sayyaaratul-waalid	سيارة الوالد
sayyaaratuT-Taalib	سيارة الطالب

6.5 Sun and moon letters

As mentioned in Chapter 1, section 4, the first letter after the definite article must be pronounced differently depending on whether it is a sun or a moon letter. Thus, what you hear is not always what you write! For example, you hear the word *as-sayyaara*, but you have to write the article alif lam ال.

as-sayyaara	السيارة
ar-radd	الرد
al-balad	البلد
al-farraasha	الفراشة

6.6 Taa marbuuTa ة after alif

Another silent letter is the occasional taa marbuuTa ة after alif. Students are often confused about whether to pronounce the letter as "at" or "ah". If the word is used individually, then the taa marbuuTa ة is pronounced "ah".

Examples:

mother-in-law	Hamaah	حماة	prayer	Salaah	صلاة
channel	qanaah	قناة	almsgiving	zakaah	زكاة
young woman	fataah	فتاة	prayer	du'aah	دعاة

We must remember, however, that the final taa marbuuTa ة is pronounced "at" when followed by another noun or pronoun. Listen to the examples online.

Listening sample 8 (online)

in his daily life	fii Hayaatihi al-yawmiya	في حياته اليومية
the Friday prayer	Salaatu'l-jum'a	صلاة الجمعة
the Sudanese Zakat Office	diiwaan az-zakaati's-suudaanii	ديوان الزكاة السوداني
al-Jazeera channel	qanaatu'l-jaziira	قناة الجزيرة

Exercise

EXERCISE 7. Mark all the words that contain silent or invisible letters in the following text.

وصل أحمد إلى مركز المدينة قادماً من بيت الحماة. كانت معه هذه الفتاة الشابة التي سألوا عنها دائماً. ذهبا إلى السوق حيث اشترت الفتاة فستاناً جديداً وكتباً. هناك قابلا صديقة أحمد ورجعوا كلهم إلى بيتهم لأنه جاء وقت الصلاة. في البيت أكلوا طعاماً خفيفاً وتفرجوا الأخبار في قناة الجزيرة ولكن بعد ذلك عاد أحمد إلى شقة عائلته راكباً سيارة الحماة.

7 Writing numbers

Writing Arabic numbers is not very difficult when you remember to write them from left to right! This is in the opposite direction to the letters. When using computer keyboards and word processing programs this is not an issue, because the cursor jumps automatically into the correct position; however, when you write by hand, you should allow ample space, especially when writing larger numbers.

Native speakers of Western languages also confuse the Arabic number five with the Western number zero, which is funny when you remember that the Arabs invented the number zero.

Examples:

صواب	خطأ	صواب	خطأ
15 = ١٥	10 = ١٠	155 = ١٥٥	100 = ١٠٠

Exercise

EXERCISE 8. Translate the sentences and write the correct numbers.

My phone number is 202-4595501. _____
In your bank account is 6,550,100.25 dirham. _____
The total is 105.05 dinar. _____
I was born in 1923. _____
In 1955 Cairo had a population of 5,505,000. _____

7.1 Two and three

The Arabic handwriting of numbers also includes a few special cases. Most notably is the writing of 2 and 3.

Western number	Printed form	Handwritten form
2	٢	٣
3	٣	٢

Note that the printed 2 and the handwritten 3 are identical. Because it can make a significant difference whether you have 2,000 or 3,000 Riyal in your bank account, it is worth checking the entire document for clues about which form was used to write it. If you recognize the printed 3 or the handwritten 2 then you can assume that this is the official form of writing in this document.

7.2 Numbering and listing items

The most common form of listing items in Arabic is with the ordinal number, as the English equivalent: first, second, third.

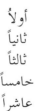

However, often the letter system is used, similar to the English a), b), c) system. For this, the Arabic alphabet was divided into eight (meaningless) sections with three or four letters each. It was argued that this was a better way to memorize and pronounce the letters. They were also given a numeric value from 1 to 1,000. The sentence below is used as a tool to help people to list items correctly according to this system.

أَبْجَد هَوَّز حُطِّي كَلِمَن سَعْفَص قُرِشَتْ ثَخَذ ضَظَغ

> **Mnemonic device**
> The Jordanian singer Umar al-Abdallat released a song by the same title that helps you to remember the letters. You can go to YouTube and search for ابجد هوز.

The following list shows the numerical value of each Arabic letter.

200	ر	20	ك	1	أ
300	ش	30	ل	2	ب
400	ت	40	م	3	ج
500	ث	50	ن	4	د
600	خ	60	س	5	ه
700	ذ	70	ع	6	و
800	ض	80	ف	7	ز
900	ظ	90	ص	8	ح
1,000	غ	100	ق	9	ط
				10	ي

8 Special cases and ligatures

In both handwriting and computer typing, some letters when connected form special ligatures or graphemes that look different from the shapes you've just learned.

Spelling الكتابة 27

Examples:

ل + م   لم
ب + ح   بح
ب + م   بم
م + ح   مح
م + م   مم
ب + ى   بى
ل + ا   لا
م + ح + م + د   محمد

Exercises

EXERCISE 9. Try for yourself!

ي + م + ح + ض _____   خ + ج + ل   _____
ل + ح + م   _____   ا + ل + أ + ل + و + ا + ن   _____
م + ح + ل   _____   ل + م + ا   _____
ن + ه + ا + ر _____   ن + ج + ي + ب   _____

9 Writing Arabic dialects

Arabic dialects are first and foremost the oral forms used for conversations and listening. As mentioned before, every Arabic native speaker communicates daily situations in his or her local dialect; even the most educated do so. Using a dialect is therefore not a measure of class or status. But how can we transmit those oral messages, lyrics and poetry into a written form, such as letters, emails, notes or text messages? This presents a major challenge because Arabic dialects use additional sounds (and sometimes letters) that are not found in the regular MSA alphabet. Some letters in MSA are pronounced differently in a dialect. Furthermore, since no official spelling rules exist, dialect writers often improvise and import letters from Persian.

tch   چ
v   ڤ
p   پ
g   گ

It is therefore not easy to find material written in dialect except in advertisements, blogs, online discussion boards, chat programs and sometimes on Twitter and other social media. Recently, a transliterated form of Arabic (known as "Arabizi") has come into use, which spells Arabic words with English (Latin) letters. This frequently occurs in chat programs or text messaging. This works for those letters that are identical, for example t, f, m; but for special Semitic letters, numbers are used as substitutes:[2]

2	ء
3	ع
'3	غ
5	خ
6	ط
'6	ظ
7	ح
8	ق
9	ص
'9	ض

Exercise

EXERCISE 10. Transliterate the Arabizi words into "real" Arabic.

7aga	_____	bitshouf 7alak fiya	_____
3an 2arib	_____	ma3ak	_____
7abibi wenta b3id	_____	la7za	_____
ya 3eny 3o2balak	_____	3ala 6ul	_____
ana rayi7 il-jami3a	_____	6aal 3umrak	_____
9ba7 il-5er	_____	i6la3	_____

---

2 Palfreyman, D. and Al Khalil, M.: "A Funky Language for Teenzz to Use: Representing Gulf Arabic in Instant Messaging", *Journal of Computer-Mediated Communication*, vol. 9, issue 1, November 2003.

3 Roots and patterns
الجذر والوزن

1 The three letter root system	30
2 How to find the root letters of an Arabic word	32
3 How to recognize a pattern of an Arabic word	33
4 How to use an Arabic–English dictionary	37

30 *Speed Up Your Arabic*

1 The three letter root system

Semitic languages like Arabic and Hebrew base the formation of their words on a system of root letters and patterns. Thus, most Arabic words have a root (or stem or origin) that consists of three letters, mostly consonants but some vowels count too. Some words have four root letters. The root expresses a general meaning and most words with the same combination of root letters are related. This system is extremely productive for word building and predicting the gist of the word. Understanding the concept of root and pattern enables students to grasp the general meaning of the word and often translate it even without the help of a dictionary. Estimates of the number of different root combinations which exist vary between 5,000 and 6,500.

Examples:

خ – ب – ط	cooking
ب – ت – ك	writing
س – ر – د	studying
ع – ط – ق	cutting
ع – م – س	listening

In order to create a specific meaning or word, the three root letters are equipped with additional markers, affixes, or letters. For each grammatical category a distinct pattern of those markers is noted, for example adjectives have certain combinations of long and short vowels and the conjugation pattern of verbs in the past tense for the second person singular masculine has specific suffixes and short vowels. In fact, all conjugations of the second person singular past tense have the same pattern. Thus, when a specific pattern meets a general root, an Arabic word is born!

Roots and patterns are the gateway to mastering Arabic and a very useful tool for students. Intimate familiarity with them allows for easy and fast reading comprehension and fluent writing. But it also helps with vocabulary learning.

Examples:

The learner learns a lesson at school (place of learning).

دَرَسَ الدارِس دِراسة في المَدْرَسة.

The writer writes a book at the office (place of writing).

كَتَبَ الكاتِب كِتاباً في المَكْتَب.

Roots and patterns الجذر والوزن

Exercise

EXERCISE 1. Recognize the general meaning of the roots and translate the sentences.

The baker bakes bread at the bakery.	خَبَزَ الخَبَّاز الخُبْز في المِخْبَز.	baking	خ - ب - ز
_____	لعب اللاعب اللعبة في الملعب.	_____	_____
_____	طبخ الطباخ الطبخ في المطبخ.	_____	_____
_____	ذبح الذباح الذبيحة في المذبحة.	_____	_____
_____	أرسل المرسِل الرسالة في المراسلة.	_____	_____
_____	زرع الزارع الزَرع في المزرعة.	_____	_____

In order to illustrate the many types of words, three example root letters were picked by the old Arab grammarians. The first example root letter is ف, the second is ع and the third is ل. Incidentally, these three letters also have a real lexical meaning ("to do"). They help us to depict the typical forms of adjectives, plurals, verbs, participles, etc.:

المثال	Description of the pattern	الوزن
جَميل، قَبيح	typical adjective pattern	فَعيل
بُيوت، دُروس	typical broken plural pattern	فُعُول
يَذْهَبُونَ، يَخْرُجُونَ	typical conjugation pattern 3rd person plural present tense Form I	يَفْعَلُونَ
طالِب، ساكِن	typical active participle pattern	فاعِل
أكَلَ، نَزَلَ	typical conjugation pattern 3rd person singular past tense Form I	فَعَلَ
مُدُن، طُرُق	typical broken plural pattern	فُعُل
اِسْتَقْبَلْتُ، اِسْتَمْتَعْتُ	typical conjugation pattern 1st person singular past tense Form X	اِسْتَفْعَلْتُ
مَدْخَل، مَصْنَع	typical pattern for locations, the place where something is done or happens	مَفْعَل
زَرْقاء، حَمْراء	typical pattern for female color adjectives	فَعْلاء

Exercise

EXERCISE 2. Based on the examples given, describe the pattern of the words below.

Description	الوزن	الترجمة	الكلمة
singular masculine adjective	فَعِيل	friendly	لطيف
_____	نُفَعِّل	we smoke	نُدَخِّن
_____	فُعَلاء	experts (masc.)	خُبَراء
_____	مُتَفَعِّلون	spectators (masc.)	مُتَفَرِّجون
_____	فُعولات	governments	حُكومات
_____	الفاعِلة	the third (fem.)	الثالِثة
_____	فَعِلوا	they failed	فَشِلوا

2 How to find the root letters of an Arabic word

Students sometimes struggle to identify the root letters. But as we have learnt, this is an essential skill and the first step in the translation process. Also, if you use the common Arabic dictionaries for translations, you will find that they are not organized alphabetically, but according to the root letters, so you will want to master this skill quickly. Here are some practical tips on how to avoid common mistakes when determining the three root letters:

1. Count the letters of the selected word. If it has only three letters, these are most likely to be your root letters, but be aware of any vowels.
2. If you have more than three letters start counting from the end of the word but omit any grammatical endings or suffixes. Now, the last letter of the word is most likely to be your third root letter. Often the second to last letter is your second root letter.
3. If the word has the article أل or ة, get rid of it.
4. Letters such as م, ت, س, or ن at the beginning of the word are often prefixes and part of the pattern, but not of the root. Thus, they should be omitted.
5. Now check for vowels. They tend to mess things up. Although ا is a common letter, it is never a root letter. و and ي, however, can be part of the root.

Roots and patterns الجذر والوزن 33

> **Tip**
> If you are trying to determine the root letters of a verb and you don't find the answer in the present tense form of the verb, check the past tense. Equally, if you are unable to identify the root letters in the singular noun, look at the plural form of the noun.

3 How to recognize a pattern of an Arabic word

After you have determined the root letters, whatever marker or letter is left is part of the pattern and helps you to determine the word type. Each word type is characterized by specific combinations of short and long vowels, prefixes and suffixes and other grammatical symbols. There is a pattern for verbs, for the tense of the verb, for the conjugation of each verb in the past and present tense, for the negation of the verb, for verbal nouns, etc. And the same is true for nouns and adjectives, marking the gender, status, and number.

Now you have identified the root (general meaning) of your word and the word type. By now you have already learnt a lot about the word, some say as much as 80 percent. With help from the context (and a dictionary if necessary) you can finish your translation easily.

Examples:

مَدْرَسَة

1 It has more than three letters.
2 The ة must go.
3 The س is my third root letter.
4 The م is a prefix and must be omitted.
5 No vowels!

The *root* of مَدْرَسَة is د - ر - س (from right to left).

The *pattern* is مَفْعَلَة: it describes a singular, feminine noun of place.

نَسْتَعِين

1 It has more than three letters.
2 There is no article or ة.
3 The final ن will be root letter number three.
4 I omit ن, س, and ت as prefixes. That leaves ع as my first root letter.

5 Now I check out the vowel, which is my second root letter. I will do this with a little help from my friend Hans Wehr, the dictionary. There I see that the root letter is actually و and not ي.

The *root* of نَسْتَعِين is ن – و – ع (from right to left).

The *pattern* is نَسْتَفْعِل: it describes a first person plural present tense of Form X.

كَانَ

1 The word only has three letters. But one is ا, which cannot be a root letter.
2 There are no other prefixes or suffixes.
3 The ن is the third root letter.
4 See step 2. ك is my first root letter.
5 The ا is a vowel, but does not count. If we cannot find the answer in this form, we look at the complementing form of the present tense يَكُون. The و is our second root letter.

The *root* of كَانَ is ن – و – ك (from right to left).

The *pattern* is فَعَلَ: it describes a third person singular past tense conjugation of a weak verb in Form I.

Exercises

EXERCISE 3. Follow the steps above to determine the root and pattern of the following words. For each word, list your steps, then give the root, the pattern and what the pattern describes.

التَفْكِير
يُساعِدونَها
الاستئجار

EXERCISE 4. Replace the root letters with the three example letters (ف-ع-ل) and vocalize the word.

الوزن	الكلمة	الوزن	الكلمة
_____	تحميل	_____	يذهب
_____	سيارة	_____	مبروك
_____	إنجازات	_____	صباح
_____	إشتراك	_____	إجتماع
_____	جدد	_____	سافرنا
_____	حقائق	_____	بحيرة

EXERCISE 5. Decide which set of root letters is correct.

الكلمة	الجذر ١	الجذر ٢	الجواب الصحيح: ١ أو ٢؟
مدارس	د – ر – س	م – ر – س	_____
خطّ	خ – ط – ء	خ – ط – ط	_____
أجهزة	أ – ه – ز	ج – ه – ز	_____
محطّة	م – ح – ط	ح – ط – ط	_____
أبيض	أ – ب – ض	ب – ي – ض	_____
صلاة	ص – ل – و	ص – ل – ا	_____
كُرة	ك – ر – ر	ك – ر – و	_____
التغيّب	ت – غ – ب	غ – ي – ب	_____
مستقبل	س – ق – ل	ق – ب – ل	_____
يضعون	ي – ض – ع	و – ض – ع	_____

EXERCISE 6. Determine the root and pattern, and write the translation.

الكلمة	الجذر	الوزن	الترجمة
الجامعة	_____	_____	_____
التدخين	_____	_____	_____
السبعينات	_____	_____	_____
المساعدة	_____	_____	_____
كانتْ	_____	_____	_____
دقائق	_____	_____	_____
يشاهدون	_____	_____	_____
إشتباكات	_____	_____	_____
وزارة	_____	_____	_____

EXERCISE 7. Use the pattern to create words and translate them.

الجذر	الوزن	الكلمة	الترجمة
خ ب ز	مَفْعَل	_____	_____
ط و ل	فَعيل	_____	_____
ز و ر	فِعَالة	_____	_____
ح س ن	أَفْعَل	_____	_____

36 *Speed Up Your Arabic*

الترجمة	الكلمة	الوزن	الجذر
_____	_____	أَفْعَال	ص ح ب
_____	_____	مُفْعِلة	و ز ن
_____	_____	افْتَعَلَتْ	ج م ع
_____	_____	فُعُول	ق ل ب
_____	_____	مُفَاعَلَة	ر ق ب
_____	_____	تَفْعِيل	د خ ن
_____	_____	فُعَلَاء	ز م ل
_____	_____	مَفْعُول	ح ب ب
_____	_____	مُفَعِّل	ص و ر
_____	_____	فُعَل	غ ر ف

EXERCISE 8. The patterns أفعال and فُعول are the most common broken plural patterns. Check the glossary and see if you can find 20 examples of each pattern.

أفعال		فُعول	
جمع التكسير	مفرد	جمع التكسير	مفرد
أهداف	هدف	ضيوف	ضيف

EXERCISE 9. Use the pattern مَفعل to create your own words of location.

الترجمة	المكان	الجذر
exit	مَخرج	خ – ر – ج
_____	_____	ل – ع – ب
_____	_____	ط – ي – ر
_____	_____	ج – ل – س
_____	_____	ن – ز – ل
_____	_____	غ – س – ل
_____	_____	ص – ر – ف
_____	_____	ع – ب – د
_____	_____	س – ب – ح
_____	_____	د – خ – ل

Roots and patterns الجذر والوزن 37

4 How to use an Arabic–English dictionary

It seems so easy to type an Arabic word into Google Translate or other translation software. And the results are not bad; however, a multi-word phrase or even a sentence gives you incomplete, incomprehensible and often incorrect answers. Thus, keep using the old-fashioned hardcopy dictionary when looking up words. But don't expect to find them in alphabetical order. Unfortunately, most Arabic–English dictionaries are not arranged in this way, but instead they follow the root letter system. If you want to look up a word in a dictionary of this kind you must first identify the three root letters and then find the entry in the book. There all the derivatives from the same root are listed together, typically the verb and its extended forms first.

Arguably the best Arabic–English dictionary is the one written by the German orientalist Hans Wehr, which was later translated into English.[1] It follows the same root system plus it gives transliterations and short vowels for the verbs. Now get ready, find the root letters, be aware of the vowels and start translating.

For the different verb forms he uses Roman numerals, but as you will quickly note there are plenty of choices, synonyms and options for translation. Don't automatically pick the first one! Skim through the list of possible translations and see which one fits your context the best. Although this leaves you with some arbitrary choices, it still works better than any online translator.

The dictionary organizes the root entries according to the following categories:

- verbs (Roman I–X, if applicable; note that the actual verb is not written in the text, only the Roman numeral)
- nouns
- adjectives
- nouns of place
- verbal nouns (المصدر) starting with Form II. Here the book does not give you the Roman numeral but the real word instead.
- active and passive participles of Forms I–X.

---

1 Hans Wehr: *Arabic–English Dictionary: The Hans Wehr Dictionary of Modern Written Arabic*. Ed. by J. Milton Cowan, Spoken Language Services, 1994.

Exercise

EXERCISE 10. Look up the following words in a dictionary. Remember to identify the root and pattern first.

الترجمة	الكلمة	الترجمة	الكلمة	الترجمة	الكلمة
_____	خضراء	_____	محطة	_____	مدارس
_____	ملحمة	_____	أصدقاء	_____	تعلمتُ
_____	إمكانيات	_____	العودة	_____	مؤسسة
_____	وسخ	_____	استيقظت	_____	اقامة
_____	يصلون	_____	بارد	_____	رواية

Just for fun, now check the translations with your favorite online translator. You will find different suggestions, especially with the verbs.

4 Nouns and adjectives
الاسم والصفة

1 Nouns الاسم	**40**
1.1 Agreement rules for number	40
1.2 Agreement rules for gender	45
1.3 Agreement rules for state	47
1.4 Agreement rules for grammatical cases	50
2 Borrowed nouns	**50**
3 iDaafa الإضافة	**51**
4 Participles اسم فاعل واسم مفعول	**53**
5 Adjectives الصفة	**56**
5.1 Agreement rules	56
5.2 Attributive or predicative use of adjectives	56
5.3 Nisba adjectives النسبة	58
5.4 Comparative and superlative	59
5.5 Color adjectives الألوان	61
6 Possessive pronouns الضمائر الملكية	**63**

40 *Speed Up Your Arabic*

Since Arabic has almost no cognates, students spend a lot of time memorizing new vocabulary. Once they realize the similarities and patterns on which Arabic words are built, this task becomes much easier. Arabic nouns are so manifold that they can be considered the largest group of words in the dictionary. If a word is not a verb or a preposition, it is most likely a noun. Adjectives are very similar to nouns, and quite often they can switch sides easily. A common definition of an Arabic noun is that it may take the definite article. It can also take the indefinite article, which in Arabic is marked by nunation (see section 1.3 below).

Aside from memorizing nouns and adjectives as new vocabulary, there are a few steps and rules to remember in order to use them properly. Among the most common problems and errors are the use of the definite article, the recognition of active and passive participles, agreement rules, and the use of the adjective either as an attribute or a predicate.

Let us first look at the extensive list of nouns and adjectives:

- verbal nouns
- participles (active and passive)
- proper nouns
- collective nouns
- nisba nouns
- diminutives
- nouns of place
- adverbs
- numbers

And here is a list of basic points to remember when using nouns and adjectives. They describe agreement rules with related words:

- number (singular, dual, plural)
- gender (masculine, feminine)
- state (definite, indefinite)
- case (nominative, genitive, accusative)

1 Nouns الاسم

1.1 Agreement rules for number

Arabic nouns and adjectives appear in three numbers: the singular (المُفرد), the dual (المُثنى), and the plural (الجمع). Adjectives agree with the noun in number, i.e. a singular noun is followed by a singular adjective. Singular (feminine) adjectives are, however, used to modify non-human plural nouns.

Nouns and adjectives الاسم والصفة 41

The singular المفرد

With either the definite or indefinite article, singular nouns represent the one-form of the Arabic noun. The singular noun can be of masculine or feminine gender.

Examples:

| a car | سيارةٌ | a book | كتابٌ |
| the car | السيارةُ | the book | الكتابُ |

The dual or two-form المثنى

Since this number does not exist in English as a separate noun category, students often forget to apply this concept and instead use the number two and the plural noun or the number two and the singular noun.

خطأ	صواب
إِثنان بيوت	بيتان
إِثنين سيارة	سيارتان

But Arabic does recognize the two-form in most parts of speech: pronouns, nouns, adjectives and verbs all take a special suffix to mark the dual. In colloquial Arabic only the dual of the noun is regularly used.

Listening sample 9 (online)

Listen to the correct pronunciation on the website.

two cars	سيارتانِ	two books	كتابانِ
the two cars	السيارتانِ	the two books	الكتابانِ
in the two cars	في السيارتَيْنِ	in the two books	في الكتابَيْنِ

The plural الجمع

Arabic has two plural forms: the sound plural (الجمع السالم), which is formed by suffixes, and the broken plural (جمع التكسير). It is estimated that half of the Arabic nouns have a sound plural and the other half have a broken plural. Finding the correct form is a difficult task for all learners. Perhaps more statistics can make it easier: about 90 percent of feminine nouns have a sound plural while only 10 percent of masculine nouns do. Most masculine nouns form a broken plural.

The sound plural has a masculine form (ونَ / ـينَ) and a feminine form (ات).

The broken plural is formed by specific patterns. At least 30 of these patterns are used frequently; some are shown here:

أفْعال، فُعْل، فواعِل، أفْعُل، فُعُل، فَعائِل، أفْعِلة، فِعَل، فَعالا، فُعّال، فِعال، فُعول، فُعَلاء، فِعال

It is very difficult to predict the correct pattern, especially when you have seemingly identical singular words, which then follow a different broken plural pattern.

Examples:

الجمع	وزن جمع التكسير	المفرد
كُرَماء	فُعَلاء	كريم
صِغار	فِعال	صغير

However, more often there is some similarity in the broken plural pattern.

Examples:

الجمع	وزن جمع التكسير	المفرد
طُلّاب	فُعّال	طالِب
كُتّاب	فُعّال	كاتِب
دُروس	فُعول	دَرْس
بُيوت	فُعول	بَيْت
أقْلام	أفْعال	قَلَم
أمْثال	أفْعال	مَثَل

Tip
When you see a feminine noun ending with taa marbuuTa ة, it is almost always correct to use the sound plural suffix, while for the masculine nouns you almost always have to memorize the broken plural form.

Remember, a general agreement between noun and adjective exists: if the noun is a singular noun then it takes a singular adjective. This agreement works for dual and plural too, except for the non-human plurals!

Nouns and adjectives الاسم والصفة 43

Plural chart for Arabic nouns:

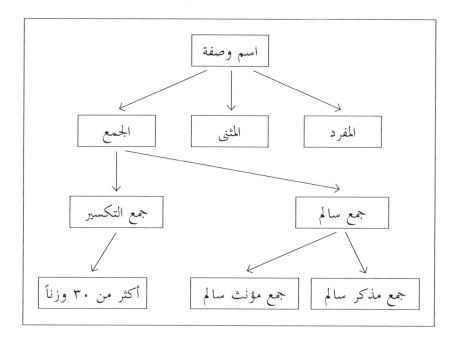

Examples:

Sound plurals

مذكر مفكّر مشهور مفكّرون مشهورون
مؤنث مفكّرة مشهورة مفكّرات مشهورات

Broken plurals

جمع التكسير	الوزن	المفرد
بُيُوت	فُعُول	بيت
أَبْوَاب	أَفْعَال	باب
طُلاب	فُعَال	طالب
كِبَار	فِعَال	كبير
قُدَمَاء	فُعَلاء	قديم

Exercises

EXERCISE 1. Mix and match the nouns and adjectives to create plural phrases.

رجل	كبير
قلم	عراقي
سيدة	مشغول
شارع	جديد
يوم	لطيف
ساعة	واسع
لغة	طويل
طالب	كثير
جامعة	أجنبي
طالبة	نشيط

EXERCISE 2. Change the sentences from singular to plural.

المفرد	الجمع
هناك بيت جديد.	هناك بيوت جديدة.
هناك مدرسة قديمة.	
في البيت غرفة كبيرة.	
الرسالة طويلة.	
الصورة جميلة.	
في الصف زميل جديد.	
هناك معيد مجتهد.	
الدرس صحيح.	
هنا صديقة جميلة.	
الغرفة نظيفة.	
سيارتك وسخة.	
في الجامعة أستاذ أجنبي.	

1.2 Agreement rules for gender

English-speaking students of Arabic often struggle with the concept of grammatical gender: classifying words into masculine and feminine categories. Since English does not follow this concept they rightly ask why one word is masculine and another is feminine.

chair – masc.   مذكر – كرسي

table – fem.   مؤنث – طاولة

Arabic nouns and adjectives have a pre-assigned gender and are thus either masculine or feminine by definition. The gender definition of the noun is extremely important because it affects surrounding and related words, such as adjectives and verbs, which have to change in order to accommodate the gender of the noun.

Usually, gender is marked clearly in Arabic. Those words ending on a taa marbuuTa ة are usually feminine. If the word does not end with a taa marbuuTa ة, is it most likely masculine, with some notable exceptions:

Some nouns are feminine by definition: شمس, حرب, يد

Some nouns are feminine because of their natural gender: أم, بنت, أخت

Some nouns end on a taa marbuuTa ة but they are not feminine: أسامة, دكاترة, أساتذة

Arabic allows you to switch gender easily. Simply adding the taa marbuuTa ة to a noun (or adjective) makes the noun a feminine noun. For example, when referring to humans, jobs or titles, we can change the gender by adding or omitting the taa marbuuTa ة.

Examples:

مؤنث	مذكر	مؤنث	مذكر
ملكة	ملك	أستاذة	أستاذ
خبيرة	خبير	جدة	جد
واحدة	واحد	جميلة	جميل

A basic gender agreement exists between noun and adjective. If the noun is masculine, the adjective must be masculine too, and if the noun is feminine, the adjective takes a taa marbuuTa ة to make it feminine. Frequently, students forget to attach the taa marbuuTa ة to the feminine adjective. This agreement rule works for singular and plural with one notable exception: plurals of non-humans.

These do not follow the gender and number agreement. Non-human plurals are treated as if they are feminine singulars (see section 1.1 above).

Examples:

الجمع	المفرد
طلاب جدد	طالب جديد
طالبات جديدات	طالبة جديدة
كتب جديدة	كتاب جديد
سيارات جديدة	سيارة جديدة

Exercises

EXERCISE 3. Mark the correct gender for the following nouns. M = masculine and F = feminine.

الجنس	الاسم	الجنس	الاسم	الجنس	الاسم
_____	الارض	_____	الوالدة	_____	كلب
_____	مُدُن	_____	ولد	_____	عمارة
_____	مترجمات	_____	جميل	_____	معلمون
_____	رجال	_____	كُتَيْبة	_____	اليوم
_____	أنْتَ	_____	الجمهورية	_____	عاصمة

EXERCISE 4. Write the correct form of the adjective.

الغرفة + وسخ _____
الرحلة + طويل _____
العدد + كبير _____
الموظفات + مشغول _____
الأكل + لذيذ _____
البيوت + بعيد _____
الدروس + صعب _____
الراتب + مناسب _____
درجة الحرارة + عالي _____
السياسيون + فاسد _____

Nouns and adjectives الاسم والصفة 47

1.3 Agreement rules for state

Arabic nouns are either in the definite or the indefinite state. The definite state is marked by the definite article ال (see Chapters 1 and 2 for more on the pronunciation of articles with sun and moon letters) or possessive pronouns, proper nouns and the إضافة. An indefinite article does not exist in Arabic. Instead a suffix called nunation is added that consists of a short vowel and the sound of the letter nuun ن. This short syllable is not written, but it does change according to the grammatical case ending (see Chapter 5, section 1).

Case	Indefinite masculine noun		Indefinite feminine noun	
Nominative	qalamun	قَلَمٌ	sayyaaratun	سيارةٌ
Genitive	qalamin	قَلَمٍ	sayyaaratin	سيارةٍ
Accusative	qalaman	قَلَماً	sayyaaratan	سيارةً

Students often struggle with the use of the article in Arabic because it is different from English. For example, Arabic does not have a visible marker for indefiniteness except for the nunation. In general, you use the article more frequently in Arabic than in English.

Examples:

الجملة الانجليزية	أل – نعم أو لا	الجملة العربية
The school is good.	نعم	المدرسة جيدة.
A school is in my area.	لا	في منطقتي مدرسة.
I am going to school.	نعم	أذهب إلى المدرسة.

> **Tip**
> Only the second example does not have an article in Arabic. Before translating, check your English sentences to see if they include "a" or "an". If they do, then you don't need an article in your Arabic sentence. Otherwise make sure you write ال.

Remember the special rule for pronouncing the article after sun and moon letters.

Note that although the first word in the إضافة is technically a definite noun, it does not carry the article (see section 3 below).

Exercise

EXERCISE 5. Listen to the sentences on the website and write in the article if needed (the full text is in the answer key).

___ مدينة ___ كبيرة   في هذا ___ محل ___ كتب ___ كثيرة

يذهب والدي إلى ___ مكتب   ___ عاصمة ___ سعودية هي ___ رياض

هناك ___ مدرسة ___ جيدة   تلبس ___ نفس ___ فستان

في ___ بيت خمس ___ غرف   ___ حكومة ___ سورية

احب أن ادرس ___ لغات   ___ جماعة ___ إخوان ___ مسلمين

يحب ___ شباب ___ رياضة   نحن في ___ بيت

تقف ___ سيارة أمام ___ بيت   ما فهمت ___ سؤالك

تشرب أختي ___ قهوة في ___ مساء   عندي ___ وقت لـ ___ ذهاب إلى ___ بحر

قضينا ___ اسبوعين في هذا ___ مكان   ___ جامعة ___ دول ___ عربية

اشاهد ___ تليفزيون في ___ صباح   يدرس ___ طلاب ___ كثيرون ___ هندسة

Proper nouns

Proper nouns are usually considered feminine definite nouns. Some nouns carry the article, while others don't. If they don't have an article, they are called diptote nouns, i.e. nouns that don't have nunation even when they are indefinite.

Tip

Unfortunately, there is no way of determining which Arab country has an article and which one does not other than a small hint: those names with a true Arabic meaning tend to have an article, while those that appear to be true proper names do not. For example, al-baHrayn literally means "the two seas" and al-maghrib means "the land of the west". Names like lubnaan or libiya cannot be traced back to an Arabic root. But exceptions apply, so you should memorize the common Arab countries and cities which have an article and those which do not.

Examples:

بعض الدول العربية ودول أخرى

المغرب   فلسطين   البحرين   أمريكا

الجزائر   الأردن   السعودية   ألمانيا

Nouns and adjectives الاسم والصفة

فرنسا	الإمارات	سوريا	تونس	
اليابان	قطر	لبنان	ليبيا	
اسبانيا	عمان	العراق	مصر	
السويد	اليمن	الكويت	السودان	

أهم المدن العربية

الدوحة	بيروت	دمشق	الرباط
مسقط	القدس	عمان	القاهرة
دبي	الرياض	بغداد	الخرطوم
صنعاء	مكة المكرمة	المدينة المنورة	أبو ظبي

Most names for cities and countries are feminine (مؤنث), with the exception of:

الأردن، السودان، العراق، المغرب، لبنان، اليمن

Exercise

EXERCISE 6. Try to recognize the names of all 21 Arab countries written in different fonts:

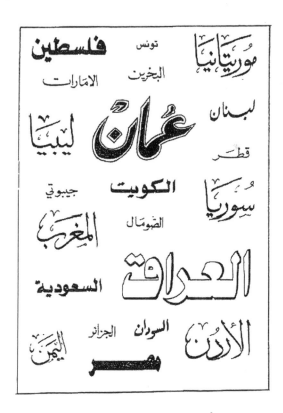

1.4 Agreement rules for grammatical cases

See Chapter 5 for more on the إِعراب.

Here is another "case" of fundamental differences between English and Arabic and the subsequent difficulties for learners of the other language. English does not recognize grammatical case markers; Arabic does. Depending on its function, the noun in a sentence takes a marker for the case. Typically, Arabic distinguishes three cases: nominative (subject case), genitive (possession and indirect objects), and accusative (direct objects and adverbs). The short vowels are used to mark the case endings: nominative = u (ُ), genitive = i (ِ) and accusative = a (َ). Nouns and adjectives can carry these case endings whether they are in the definite or indefinite state. To distinguish indefinite case endings, the sound of the letter noun ن is added. This is called nunation and it creates the following endings: indefinite nominative = un (ٌ), indefinite genitive = in (ٍ), and indefinite accusative = an (ً).

Note that the indefinite accusative for nouns not ending in a taa marbuuTa ة (most masculine singulars and broken plurals) is marked by writing the letter alif at the end of the word (ًا).

Examples:

البيتُ الجديدُ / بيتٌ جديدٌ

في البيتِ الجديدِ / في بيتٍ جديدٍ

اشترى البيتَ الجديدَ / اشترى بيتاً جديداً.

For daily speech, these endings are mostly irrelevant. Exceptions include the noun–possessive pronoun phrase, some sound masculine plurals and some adverbs.

2 Borrowed nouns

See also Chapter 9.

The number of loan words from other languages in the Arabic language is small. In the past, some Persian, Aramaic or Turkish words found their way into the mostly oral vernacular. In recent times, however, English words have become an active component of written and spoken Arabic forms because of the position of English as the language of science and the language of the cool kids.

As mentioned earlier, the number of cognates and subsequently the number of false friends in Arabic is very small. Only a handful of words actually made it into MSA through loan translations (and a few more into local dialects). Such

Nouns and adjectives الاسم والصفة 51

words can be recognized by their different structure. They don't look like regular Arabic words with a root, a long vowel, an article or an affix. However, it is surprising to see how often we stumble over these words, not recognizing their foreign origin. This happens frequently when foreign proper names are transcribed in Arabic.

Exercise

EXERCISE 7. Quickly and without much preparation read and translate the following words:

انجليزي	عربي	انجليزي	عربي
_____	لندن	_____	واشنطن
_____	أوروبّا	_____	اوبريت
_____	تليفون	_____	ايميل
_____	اتوبيس	_____	فيتامينات
_____	كافيتريا	_____	دكتور

The "real" cognates, however, act like Arabic nouns, i.e. they follow the agreement rules, take an article, switch to plural, and are integrated into patterns, etc.

Examples:

satellite (*lit.*: industrial moon)
قمر صناعي
vacuum cleaner (*lit.*: electrical broom)
مكنسة كهربائية
cigarette
سيجارة
parliament
البرلمان

democracy
الديموقراطية
strategy
الاستراتيجية
email (*lit.*: electronic message)
الرسالة الإلكترونية
Native Americans (*lit.* Red Indians)
الهنود الحمر

3 iDaafa الإضافة

A common way in Arabic to express possession is through the إضافة construction. إضافة means "adding something" (المُضيف إليه) and is the equivalent of the English phrase "the house of my family", i.e. "my family's house". The إضافة connects two or more nouns with each other. Two, three and occasionally four nouns express phrases such as: "The flat tire of the car of my brother" or "The long lecture of the president of the country".

52 Speed Up Your Arabic

Tip
Students often wrongly switch the words in the إضافة. When they hear "my brother's car" they often translate أ, سيارة أخي, because it seems easier to use the same word order in Arabic. They also often add the preposition من "from", thinking it means "of", i.e. the car of my brother, سيارة من أخي. However, as we have learned, the word order in the إضافة is the opposite and does not need a preposition. I still think using the English version that includes the preposition "of" is a good idea, i.e. instead of saying "my brother's car" say "the car of my brother". This makes the translation into Arabic much easier because the Arabic phrase has the same word order, سيارة أخي. But please remember not to translate "of".

Chart for إِضافة :

اسم ١ + اسم ٢	noun 1 + noun 2
المضاف + المضاف اليه	the possessed noun + the possessor
السيارة + أخي	the car + my brother
سيارة أخي	the car of my brother (my brother's car)

Note the use of the definite article in English. It is the same as in the إضافة: nouns in the إضافة are usually definite although they do not show the signs of definite nouns. The rules say that only the last noun in the إضافة takes the article while the first (and second and third) don't. They are, however, still considered definite nouns and must be used as such.

Exercises

EXERCISE 8. Combine the words from the two columns to create a meaningful إِضافة.

_____	البرلمان	مكتب
_____	العالم	رقم
_____	الرئيس	عضو
_____	الشركة	عاصمة
_____	المقالة	سعر
_____	تليفوني	نهاية

Nouns and adjectives الاسم والصفة 53

_____	زوجة الدولة
_____	مدير كيلو سكر
_____	ملخص المباراة
_____	كأس أخي

Note that إضافة is a very stable word combination. It is very uncommon to place any attribute or other modifiers between the two segments. Adjectives describing the first word in the إضافة should go to the end of the phrase. Only in cases of obvious confusion should the إضافة be split by using the preposition لِ.

Examples:

my brother's new car	سيارة أخي الجديدة
my little brother's car	سيارة أخي الصغير
my little brother's new car	السيارة الجديدة لأخي الصغير

Exercise

EXERCISE 9. Which of the following phrases are إضافة?

	خطأ أو صواب	إضافة
_____		كلية الهندسة
_____		مدينة الكويت
_____		بيته الجميل
_____		مناقشة سبل التعاون
_____		المدينة المنورة
_____		رئيس الوزراء
_____		غرفة نوم
_____		دولة قطر
_____		أستاذ جامعي
_____		الجامعة العربية

4 Participles اسم فاعل واسم مفعول

Participles are types of nouns or adjectives that are derivates from Arabic verbs. Especially in spoken Arabic, both MSA and colloquial, they are used frequently.

54 *Speed Up Your Arabic*

However, students tend to omit them, mostly because they prefer using the equivalent verb.

We distinguish between the active participle اسم فاعل and the passive participle اسم مفعول. The active participle refers to the active agent or doer of the action word.

Examples:

player	لاعِب	Mufti	مُفْتي	writer	كاتب
reporter	مُراسِل	owner	مالِك	student	طالِب
reader	قارئ	graduate	مُتَخَرِّج	teacher	مُدَرِّس

The passive participle refers to the undergoer, recipient or result of the action.

Examples:

chosen	مُختار	responsible	مَسؤول	known	مَعروف
understood	مَفْهوم	project	مَشروع	broken	مُكَسَّر
used	مُسْتَعْمَل	selected (team)	مُنْتَخَب	grilled	مَشوي

Most participles are used as regular nouns or adjectives; some can be used as both. That means all relevant rules for nouns and adjectives apply to them (see Chapter 6, section 3). Theoretically, they can be derived from any of the famous verb patterns; however, as a rule of thumb, active participles are more common than passive. But both usually describe a state and not an event. To describe events we should still use the regular verb.

Example chart for active and passive participles of the most common verbal patterns:

اسم مفعول	اسم فاعل	المضارع	الماضي	الوزن
مَفْعُول	فاعِل	يَفْعَل	فَعَلَ	I
مُفَعَّل	مُفَعِّل	يُفَعِّل	فَعَّلَ	II
مُفَاعَل	مُفَاعِل	يُفاعِل	فَاعَلَ	III
مُفْعَل	مُفْعِل	يُفْعِل	أفْعَلَ	IV
مُتَفَعَّل	مُتَفَعِّل	يَتَفَعَّل	تَفَعَّلَ	V
مُتَفَاعَل	مُتَفَاعِل	يَتَفَاعَل	تَفَاعَلَ	VI
مُنْفَعَل	مُنْفَعِل	يَنْفَعِل	انْفَعَلَ	VII
مُفْتَعَل	مُفْتَعِل	يَفْتَعِل	افْتَعَلَ	VIII
مُسْتَفْعَل	مُسْتَفْعِل	يَسْتَفْعِل	اسْتَفْعَلَ	X

Nouns and adjectives الاسم والصفة 55

Remember that irregular (hollow, defective) verbs with vowel root letters follow slightly different patterns.

Note that without vocalization it is often impossible to distinguish between active and passive participles of the derived forms!

Exercises

EXERCISE 10. Derive the active participles from the following verbs.

اسم فاعل	الفعل الماضي	اسم فاعل	الفعل الماضي
_____	قتل	_____	سافر
_____	خاف	_____	وقع
_____	ساعد	_____	تحدث
_____	استثمر	_____	استعمل
_____	شاهد	_____	بحث

EXERCISE 11. Derive the passive participles from the following verbs.

اسم مفعول	الفعل الماضي	اسم مفعول	الفعل الماضي
_____	ذكر	_____	شرع
_____	اشترك	_____	الحق
_____	وضع	_____	قصد
_____	لوّن	_____	استعمل

EXERCISE 12. Form the appropriate active or passive participle from the given verbs.

١) التدخين _____ (يمنع) في هذه الغرفة.
٢) يقع المطعم _____ (يخرج) سور المدينة القديمة.
٣) السيد فرحان هو ال _____ (ينطق) الرسمي لمجلس الشورى.
٤) أنا _____ (يتزوج) منذ عشر سنين.
٥) بعد التخرج أشتغل _____ (يُعيد) في نفس الكلية.
٦) اللاعب سامي جابر هو _____ (يلعب) _____ (يشهر) في ال _____ (ينتخب) السعودي.
٧) صديقتي ريم هي _____ (يسكن) مع أسرتها في دبي.

٨) أمس شاهدتُ فلماً مع ال _____ (يمثّل) ال _____ (يعرف) عادل امام.

٩) أمي _____ (يعرف) أنا _____ (ينام).

١٠) الوضع في مصر _____ (يختلف) عن الوضع السوري.

١١) عفواً، الأخ عبد الله _____ (وجد)؟

١٢) نعم، ولكن هو _____ (يشغل).

١٣) هذه الطماطم _____ (يستورد) من كندا.

١٤) الشركة ال _____ (يستورد) _____ (يقيم) في دبي.

١٥) المكتبة _____ (يفتح) كل يوم حتى الساعة التاسعة.

5 Adjectives الصفة

5.1 Agreement rules

A common mistake for English-speaking learners of Arabic is to place the adjective in front of the noun. They also tend to confuse the two functions of the adjective: attributive and predicative. In Arabic, this is associated with the use of the definite article. As said earlier, adjectives are very similar to nouns, in that they conform to gender and number rules. However, the use of the adjective is always dependent on the noun.

5.2 Attributive or predicative use of adjectives

Adjectives have two functions: attributive and predicative. The attributive adjective is part of a noun phrase, where it follows the noun and agrees with it in number, gender, and status.

Examples:

the new car	السيارة الجديدة
a new car	سيارة جديدة
the difficult situation	الوضع الصعب
a difficult situation	وضع صعب

When used as a predicate, the adjective is part of a nominal sentence without a verb. It still agrees with the noun in number and gender, but usually does not carry an article.

Nouns and adjectives الاسم والصفة   57

Examples:

The car is new.   السيارة جديدة.

The situation is difficult.   الوضع صعب.

It is possible and common to combine the two forms:

The new car is expensive.   السيارة الجديدة غالية.

The new situation is difficult.   الوضع الجديد صعب.

Do not forget the agreement rules for number, gender and status.

Different rules apply for nouns describing non-human beings or things. Then the adjective takes the feminine singular form for both the attributive and the predicative function. Memorize the following rule as it is different from English and one of the most commonly violated.

Non-human plurals are treated like feminine singulars!

Examples:

The (male) students are smart.   الطلاب أذكياء.

The (female) students are smart.   الطالبات ذكيات.

The cars are expensive.   السيارات غالية.

The situations are difficult.   الأوضاع صعبة.

Exercise

EXERCISE 13. Translate the attributive or predicative use of the adjective.

_____   هذا بيت قديم.

_____   هذا البيت قديم.

_____   هذا البيت القديم

_____   هذا البيت القديم نظيف.

This is a great idea.   _____

This idea is great.   _____

this great idea   _____

This great idea is unique.   _____

58 *Speed Up Your Arabic*

هذه كتب غالية.

هذه الكتب غالية.

هذه الكتب الغالية

هذه الكتب الغالية نادرة.

These are young men. _____

These men are young. _____

these young men _____

These young men are brave. _____

5.3 Nisba adjectives النسبة

Aside from the common فَعيل pattern, adjectives are also derived from nouns by adding the nisba ending. The ending is ـيّ for masculine adjectives and ـيّة for feminine. This is a very popular mechanism to create words and phrases, especially ones related to names of places or institutions.

In only two steps, you can create your own nisba adjective:

1 Remove the article at the beginning of the noun as well as the taa marbuuTa ة, and/or long alif ا at the end.
2 Add ـيّ to create a masculine adjective or ـيّة for a feminine one.

Examples:

Nisba adjective	النسبة		الاسم
Cairene	قاهري / قاهرية	قاهر	القاهرة
Syrian	سوري / سورية	سوري	سوريا
political	سياسي / سياسية	سياس	سياسة

Nisba adjectives referring to humans usually take the sound plural with some notable exceptions.

الجمع	المفرد
سعوديون / سعوديات	سعودي / سعودية
صحفيون / صحفيات	صحفي / صحفية
عرب / عربيات	عربي / عربية
أكراد / كرديات	كردي / كردية
صيادلة / صيدليات	صيدلي / صيدلية

Nouns and adjectives الاسم والصفة

Exercise

EXERCISE 14. First derive the nisba from the noun, and then use the adjective appropriately in the sentence.

١) الحروف ــــــــ وــــــــ. (الشمس، القمر)

٢) الوضع ــــــــ في اليونان صعب جدا. (الاقتصاد)

٣) هذا الجهاز من انتاج ــــــــ. (الصين)

٤) العلاقات ــــــــ بين البلدين جيدة. (التجارة)

٥) طرابلس الشرق مدينة ــــــــ وطرابلس الغرب مدينة ــــــــ. (لبنان، ليبيا)

٦) والدي كان عنده سكتة ــــــــ. (القلب)

٧) دراسات العالم ــــــــ و ــــــــ. (العرب، الإسلام)

٨) عبد الرحمن وأحمد وخالد شباب ــــــــ. (السعودية)

٩) كلية العلوم ــــــــ. (السياسة)

١٠) الجملة ــــــــ والجملة ــــــــ. (الاسم، الفعل)

5.4 Comparative and superlative

The distinction between the comparative and superlative forms in Arabic does not usually present difficulties for students except where it concerns word order. Arabic knows only one form of comparison, the so-called elative. It is used to express both the comparative and the superlative. The pattern of the elative is أَفْعَلُ, which does not change and does not have to follow the agreement rules. The distinction between the comparative and superlative is based on word order. The superlative form precedes the noun; the comparative form follows it.

Examples:

Superlative: the largest country: أكبر دولة

السعودية أكبر دولة في الجزيرة العربية.

Note that the superlative is a noun and functions as the first part of an إضافة.

Comparative: a larger country: دولة أكبر

Note that the comparative is an adjective (so it follows the noun) and often includes the preposition مِن "than".

السعودية دولة أكبر من العراق.

Note that some adjectives cannot take the أَفْعَل form, such as participles, nisba adjectives and adjectives with the pattern فَعْلان. The comparative and superlative of these adjectives are formed with the phrase أَكْثَر + noun with tanwiin of fatHa. For the non-native student it is difficult to decide which noun should be used. However, because these phrases are rare, only some common forms are listed in the example below:

popular	شعبي
more popular	أكثر شعبيةً
the most popular films	الأفلام الأكثر شعبيةً
hungry	جوعان
hungrier	أكثر جوعاً
the hungriest boy	الولد الأكثر جوعاً
effective	مؤثر
more effective	أشد تأثيراً
the most effective method	المنهج الأشد تأثيراً

Exercises

EXERCISE 15. Create the elative of the following adjectives.

_____	مجتهد	_____	جميل
_____	سعيد	_____	صعب
_____	شعبي	_____	بارد
_____	عطشان	_____	صغير
_____	حارّ	_____	جديد
_____	واسع	_____	حسن

Nouns and adjectives الاسم والصفة 61

EXERCISE 16. Translate the superlative phrases.

the best class	_____
_____	أجمل بنت
the hardest decision	_____
_____	أطول عمارة
the last time	_____
_____	أجدّ سيارة
the strangest thing	_____
_____	أبعد مكان
the easiest test	_____
_____	أكبر مدينة

EXERCISE 17. Read the following text, identify all the adjectives and elatives (15 in total), and assign them to their appropriate heading.

سامر شاب طويل جدا، هو أطول من وليد ولكن خليل هو الأطول بين أصحابه. سامر أيضاً رفيع جداً، هو أرفع من صالح وهو الشاب الأطول في الصف. سامر يجلس على كرسي كبير. هذا الكرسي أكبر من الكرسي الذي يجلس عليه وليد. سامر وسيم ولكن تقول البنات إن وليد أوسم منه، وصالح هو الأوسم. المشكلة هي سامر ممتع ووليد ممل وصالح هو أكثر مللاً من وليد، في الصراحة صالح هو الأكثر مللاً في الصف كله.

Regular adjective	Comparative form	Superlative form
_____	_____	_____
_____	_____	_____
_____	_____	_____

5.5 Color adjectives الألوان

In conversation class students often complain that they do not know the colors in Arabic or that they are introduced at a very late stage. The reason for this is that color adjectives have a slightly different pattern from regular adjectives. Some color adjectives and other adjectives describing physical characteristics are formed with the same pattern as the comparatives: أَفْعَلُ. They have, however, unique feminine and plural forms.

الترجمة	جمع	مفرد مؤنث	مفرد مذكر
white	بيض / بيضاوات	بيضاء	أبيض
black	سود / سوداوات	سوداء	أسود
red	حمر / حمراوات	حمراء	أحمر
blue	زرق / زرقاوات	زرقاء	أزرق
blind	عمي / عماوات	عمياء	أعمى
stupid	حمقى / حمقاوات	حمقاء	أحمق

Other color adjectives take the more familiar pattern of the nisba adjectives:

الترجمة	جمع	مفرد مؤنث	مفرد مذكر
gray	رماديون / رماديات	رمادية	رمادي
purple	بنفسجيون / بنفسجيات	بنفسجية	بنفسجي
orange	برتقاليون / برتقاليات	برتقالية	برتقالي
pink	زهريون / زهريات	زهرية	زهري
golden	ذهبيون / ذهبيات	ذهبية	ذهبي
silver	فضيون / فضيات	فضية	فضي
colorful	ملونون / ملونات	ملونة	ملون

Color adjectives are used in many proverbs, phrases and geographical names. See Chapter 9, section 5.

Exercise

EXERCISE 18. Add the correct color adjectives.

التفاحة + red and yellow _____
الموزة + yellow _____
السماء + blue _____
الضفدع + green _____
الفيل + gray _____
البرتقال + orange _____
الدب + brown _____
العلم السعودي + green and white _____
الشعر + blond _____
العيون + blue _____

Nouns and adjectives الاسم والصفة   63

6 Possessive pronouns الضمائر الملكية

Unlike its English counterpart, the Arabic possessive pronoun is attached directly to the noun it describes. Students usually retain the rules quickly with the notable exception of adding possessive pronouns to feminine nouns. The possessive pronoun is attached directly to the masculine noun with a connecting short vowel. Feminine nouns ending on the taa marbuuTa ة change their pronunciation by adding the syllable "at" plus the connecting short vowel and the possessive pronoun. In writing, the taa marbuuTa ة becomes a real letter taa ت.

For personal pronouns see Chapter 6, section 1 and for object pronouns see Chapter 6, section 6.

English translation	Possessive pronoun with feminine noun	Possessive pronoun with masculine noun
my house/room	غرفتي	بيتي
your (masc.) house/room	غرفتُكَ	بيتُكَ
your (fem.) house/room	غرفتُكِ	بيتُكِ
his house/room	غرفتُهُ	بيتُهُ
her house/room	غرفتُها	بيتُها
our house/room	غرفتُنا	بيتُنا
your (plural) house/room	غرفتُكم	بيتُكم
their house/room	غرفتُهُم	بيتُهُم

Another common mistake is adding the article to a noun that already has a possessive pronoun.

Examples:

صواب	خطأ
بيتك	البيتك
في غرفتهم	في الغرفتهم
مع صديقي	مع الصديقي

Note that if the pronoun of the third person masculine singular and plural are preceded by an "i" sound (kasra), the short vowel of the pronoun changes from u (Damma) to i (kasra).

Listening sample 10 (online)

Listen to the examples on the website.

his house	baytuhu	بيتُهُ
in his house	fii baytihi	في بيتِهِ
in it	fiihi	فيهِ
their teachers	asaatidhatuhum	أساتذتُهُم
with their teachers	biasaatidhatihim	بأساتذتِهِم
with them	bihim	بِهِم

Exercises

EXERCISE 19. Whose is it? Combine the noun with the pronoun.

(سيارة + أنتَ) سريعة جداً. _____

(والد + نحن) مشغول دائماً. _____

(أقارب + هي) من القدس. _____

قال (لـ + هو): كيف (حال + أنت)؟ _____

هل (بيت + أنتم) قريب من (بيت + أنا)؟ _____

ليست (غرفة + أنتِ) نظيفة! _____

نسيتُ (شنطة + أنا) في السيارة. _____

(أصدقاء + نحن) من المغرب. _____

أين يسكن (عم + أنتم)؟ _____

(صوت + هي) جميل. _____

EXERCISE 20. Before you translate the following text with the help of a dictionary, mark all the plural nouns (22), then the iDaafas (7) and finally the possessive/object pronouns (6).

شيد الأنباط العرب في جنوب الأردن حضارة رائعة في القرنين الأول قبل الميلاد، وكانت مدينة البتراء التي نحتوها في الصخر من أروع ما تركوه، فقد نحتوا المعابد والقصور والمقابر، وشقوا طريقا يوصل إلى هذه المدينة يبلغ طوله ٢ كم، وهو الطريق المعروف بالسيق.

وفي البتراء عدد من الواجهات المعمارية والفنية الرائعة المنحوتة. برزت على هذه الواجهات تماثيل لأشخاص يصعب تحديد هويتهم بسبب التآكل والخراب، كما نحتت صور الطيور والأسود واقفة في القمة تحمي هذا البناء.

أما في وسط المدينة فيشاهد الزائر مئات المعالم التي حفرها وأنشأها الإنسان، من أضرحة ملكية إلى مدرج كبير وبيوت صغيرة وكبيرة وقاعات احتفالات وقنوات ماء وحمامات إضافة إلى الأسواق والبوابات.

5 Speaking Arabic properly
الإعراب

1 The case system	68
2 The nominative المرفوع	69
3 The genitive المجرور	70
4 The accusative المنصوب	71
5 Special cases	72
5.1 الإعراب for sound plurals	72
5.2 الإعراب for broken plurals	73
5.3 الإعراب for dual nouns	74

الإعراب means nothing less than speaking Arabic properly. But does it mean that we didn't speak Arabic properly before? Yes and no. Remember the issue of diglossia, the existence of two vernaculars in one language, which Arabic is known for, the age-old struggle between MSA and the various dialects. Also bear in mind that MSA is not a spoken language per se; every Arab speaks in his or her local dialect. But when talking to speakers of other dialects and on formal occasions Arabs (and non-native speakers) use MSA.

You, as a non-native speaker trying to get a good command of the language, are most likely to start with MSA. There are those who say that it is better to start with a dialect; however, there are disadvantages to this approach, most notably the fact that you have to limit yourself to one area of the Arab world. Which Arabic dialect will you pick? And secondly, reaching an advanced level in a particular dialect is hard and time-consuming. Without living there and immersing yourself in the culture, you will find it difficult to recognize the fine tunings of sarcasm, humor, anger, and local flavor. Thus, I recommend that you get a good command of MSA first and then familiarize yourself with some major dialects, perhaps one or two.

Only when Arabs from different regions come together or at formal and official functions will they speak MSA. MSA can be called the lingua franca of the Arabs, because Arabs from Iraq can use it to communicate with Arabs from Oman and Morocco. MSA is also the formal and official written form of Arabic. Any publication, anything written should be done in MSA. It derived from the language of the Quran, which is called Classical Arabic. Children all over the Arab world learn MSA in school. And what they learn is how to speak, write and read it properly. The rules for MSA were set centuries ago and modified during the Arab renaissance in the late nineteenth to early twentieth century. If you listen to speeches by presidents and kings or read novels and short stories or follow the news on al-Jazeera, they all use MSA (and sometimes add some local flavor to it). In reality, MSA and the dialects frequently mix, depending on the occasion. However, الإعراب is an outward sign that the speaker knows the rules of the game. You have learned and reviewed many rules in this book. This chapter deals with the case endings of nouns and adjectives. It is a field that requires special attention because a little short vowel can indicate whether you speak Arabic properly or not. Students of الإعراب often struggle with the details and frequently mix up the case endings. What is crucial in order to master الإعراب is a good command of basic linguistics: word type and word order, what is the subject or the object of the sentence, what is a direct object or an adverb? If you understand these concepts in your mother tongue, you will find it easy to apply them to Arabic.

1 The case system

Arabic texts are usually unvocalized, i.e. they do not show the short vowels that are so important for proper reading. Exceptions are important religious texts, such as the Quran or the Bible as well as children's books. Here you see markers for correct pronunciation and for the grammatical function of each word. These markers are our three short vowels: fatHa, Damma and kasra. If you read novels or even scientific papers, or if you listen to the news or the latest reports from the stock market, you will always hear the short vowels at the ends of the words. And if you listen carefully, you will also hear them as the final syllable of nouns and adjectives. Of course they are omitted in script but they are necessary to define the function of each word in the sentence and to allow for faster, coherent pronunciation.

Arabic recognizes three cases, which are sometimes compared to the Western grammatical cases of nominative, genitive and accusative. Depending on its function in the sentence as subject or object, the noun (and adjective) takes a marker to identify the case. Our three short vowels fatHa, Damma and kasra do exactly that, they mark the case of the noun: Damma marks the subject of the sentence, fatHa the direct object and kasra the indirect object.

Examples:

the new car (subject)	السيارةُ الجديدةُ
I bought the new car. (direct object)	اشتريت السيارةَ الجديدةَ.
in the new car (indirect object)	في السيارةِ الجديدةِ

Note that these are the endings for definite nouns. For indefinite nouns simply add the letter nuun (only for pronunciation and not in writing.) We call this *nunation*, where the ending changes to **-un**, **-an**, and **-in**.

Examples:

a new car (indef. subject)	سيارةٌ جديدةٌ
I bought a new car. (indef. direct object)	اشتريت سيارةً جديدةً.
in a new car (indef. indirect object)	في سيارةٍ جديدةٍ

I recommend that you say these endings in a way similar to the way news broadcasters use them. This will eventually increase your reading speed because you will connect the words into a string without breaks or interruptions. Please note that the case endings at the end of a sentence or separate section within a sentence are omitted.

Exercise

EXERCISE 1. Decide which form is correct: with nunation or without.

مكتبٌ كبيرٌ أو مكتبٌ كبيرٌ _____

في المحلِ أو في المحلِ _____

اشتريت شنطةً جديدةً أو اشتريت شنطةً جديدةً _____

مع أخي الصغيرِ أو مع أخي الصغيرِ _____

بعد الحربِ الباردةِ أو بعد الحربِ الباردةِ _____

الحديقةُ العامةُ أو الحديقةُ العامةُ _____

حفظ الكلماتِ الجديدةَ أو حفظ الكلماتِ الجديدةً _____

قرأت المقالةَ أو قرأت المقالةَ _____

2 The nominative المرفوع

The nominative or Damma case is used to identify the subject of the sentence. In the equational sentence (the one without verbs) both the subject and the predicate are in the nominative.

Examples:

The new car is expensive.	السيارةُ الجديدةُ غاليةٌ.
The car stopped in front of the house.	وقفتْ السيارةُ أمام البيت.
His car does not work.	سيارتُه لا تعمل.
This is a great car.	إنها سيارةٌ رائعةٌ.

Exercise

EXERCISE 2. Identify the words that take the nominative and add the vocalization.

١) الأستاذ الجديد وطلابه

٢) أعلنت الحكومة السورية بيانا رسميا

٣) المتحف الجديد في أبو ظبي واسع وحديث.

٤) هل الرواتب في بلادك مناسبة؟

٥) سيارته الجديدة غالية جدا.

٦) كرة السلة هوايته المفضلة.

٧) الأكل العربي أكل لذيذ وصحي.
٨) زوجها سعودي.
٩) هذه القصة القصيرة الجديدة بديعة.
١٠) يلعب الولد وكلبه في الحديقة.

3 The genitive المجرور

The genitive or kasra case marks indirect objects, i.e. those nouns and adjectives following prepositions.

Mnemonic device
The Arabic word for "preposition" is حرف جرّ. This helps you remember that the genitive must be used after a preposition and is also called the prepositional case, المجرور.

It is also the marker for the إضافة, where the second (or third or fourth) word in the إضافة takes the genitive ending.

Examples:

The professor's car parks in front of the family's home.	سيارةُ الأستاذِ تقف أمام بيتِ العائلةِ.
Good bye! (*lit.* "with safety")	مع السلامةِ!
I went to the city center by car.	ذهبتُ إلى مركزِ المدينةِ بسيارةٍ.
I met all the participants at the conference.	تعرفتُ على جميعِ المشاركينَ في المؤتمرِ.

Exercise

EXERCISE 3. Identify the words that take the genitive and add the vocalization.

١) ذهبنا من بيتنا القديم إلى شقتنا الجديدة بسيارة ابن العم.
٢) أجابت على جميع الأسئلة.
٣) بيت العائلة قريب من مركز المدينة.
٤) سافر مدير الشركة إلى المعرض الدولي في العاصمة.

Speaking Arabic properly الإعراب 71

٥) يتخرج معظم الطلاب من الجامعة بعد فترة دراسية من أربع سنوات.

٦) في الطابق الثالث غرفة نوم.

٧) مدرسة المدرس بعيدة عن بيت أسرته.

٨) التقى رئيس الدولة بنظيره في مؤتمر جامعة الدول العربية.

٩) أكتب بقلم رصاص في الدفتر.

١٠) من أهم الثروات الطبيعية الموجودة في المنطقة.

Tip
The genitive/prepositional case is the most obvious. Wherever you find a preposition, use المجرور with the following noun!

The genitive ending affects the pronunciation of some possessive pronouns, i.e. the third person singular (masc.) and plural (masc. and fem.). See Chapter 4, section 6.

4 The accusative المنصوب

The accusative case or fatHa case marks direct objects and adverbs. Remember to write the alif with the indefinite accusative of masculine singular nouns and broken plurals.

Examples:

I bought a new house.

اشتريتُ بيتاً جديداً.

She studied the Arabic language well.

درستْ اللغةَ العربيةَ جيداً.

Our team lost the game and the player after the red card.

خسر منتخبُنا المباراةَ واللاعبَ بعد البطاقةِ الحمراء.

He stole some treasure and sold the gold at night.

سرق كنزاً وباع الذهبَ ليلاً.

He finished his work early.

خلص أعمالَهُ مبكراً.

Exercise

EXERCISE 4. Identify the words that take the accusative and add the vocalization.

١) اشترينا كتابا عربيا ودفترا واقلاما والألبوم الجديد.

٢) في المقهى لقيتُ البنت اللبنانية وصاحبتها.

٣) دخل الصف متأخرا.

٤) حضروا محاضرة في الجامعة كل يوم.

٥) أنجزت واجباتها الكثيرة وبعد ذلك كتبت رسالة.

٦) عمل أستاذا العام الماضي.

٧) كان مريضا ولكنه أنجز واجباته.

٨) نأكل الفطور صباحا.

٩) أستمع إلى هذه المطربة دائما لأني أحب صوتها كثيرا.

١٠) شاهدوا المباريات يوم الأحد.

> **Tip**
> Usually, Arabic words do not end on the letter alif. So, if you see a word with an alif at the end, the chances are high that the noun takes the accusative case! The alif is the marker for indefinite nouns in this case.

Note that the accusative is also used for a number of other grammatical functions, for example numbers, adverbs of time and place, circumstantial and exceptional sentences, specifications and intensifications, after أَنَّ, إِنَّ, لِأَنَّ, لكنَّ, for exclamations and for general negation.

5 Special cases

5.1 الإعراب for sound plurals

The case endings for sound masculine plurals are as follows:

Case	معرف	منكر
Nominative	اَلْمُتَرْجِمُونَ	مُتَرْجِمُونَ
Genitive	اَلْمُتَرْجِمِينَ	مُتَرْجِمِينَ
Accusative	اَلْمُتَرْجِمِينَ	مُتَرْجِمِينَ

Speaking Arabic properly الإعراب 73

The case endings for sound feminine plurals are as follows:

Case	معرف	منكر
Nominative	ٱلْمُتَرْجِمَاتُ	مُتَرْجِمَاتٌ
Genitive	ٱلْمُتَرْجِمَاتِ	مُتَرْجِمَاتٍ
Accusative	ٱلْمُتَرْجِمَاتِ	مُتَرْجِمَاتٍ

Exercise

EXERCISE 5. Write the sound plurals and the grammatical endings of the following phrases.

الإعراب والجمع السالم	مفرد
_____	متفرّج + كثير
_____	طالبة + مجتهدة
_____	سياسي + فاسد
_____	مع المدرّسة الجديدة
_____	مع ناشط تونسي
_____	قابلتُ مثقفاً عراقياً
_____	لاعب + مميز
_____	تعمل في هذا المستشفى طبيبة مصرية.
_____	نحتفل العيد مع المسلم الاميركي.
_____	استقبلتْ تركيا لاجئاً سورياً.

5.2 الإعراب for broken plurals

Generally, the broken plural takes the same ending as the singular.

Case	جمع مكسر معرف	جمع مكسر منكر	مفرد
Nominative	ٱلْبُيُوتُ	بُيُوتٌ	بَيْتٌ
Genitive	ٱلْبُيُوتِ	بُيُوتٍ	بَيْتٍ
Accusative	ٱلْبُيُوتَ	بُيُوتاً	بَيْتاً

Exercise

EXERCISE 6. Give the broken plurals and their endings for the following phrases.

الترجمة	الإعراب وجمع التكسير
I bought new notebooks.	_____
many trees	_____
They live in expensive apartments.	_____
The city is known for its clean streets.	_____
after a few days	_____
There are many old mosques in the area.	_____

5.3 الإعراب for dual nouns

Case	المثنى المؤنث	المثنى المذكر
Nominative	(أل) سيارتانِ	(أل) طالبانِ
Genitive	(أل) سيارتَيْنِ	(أل) طالبَيْنِ
Accusative	(أل) سيارتَيْنِ	(أل) طالبَيْنِ

Exercise

EXERCISE 7. Choose the correct case ending for the dual.

بعد ساعتان أو بعد ساعتين _____
هناك فتاتان جميلتان أو هناك فتاتين جميلتين _____
يغضب من الوالدان أو يغضب من الوالدين _____
استأجرت شقتان أو استأجرت شقتين _____
قرأت الكتاب مرتان أو قرأت الكتاب مرتين _____
السؤالان الصعبان أو السؤالين الصعبين _____

Speaking Arabic properly الإعراب

> **Tip**
>
> In order to find the correct ending it is necessary to determine the function of the word in the sentence: whether it is the subject or the object. We can use the following question words:
>
> - The subject answers the "who?" question: Who is doing something?
> - The direct object answers the "what/whom?" question after the verb: What has been done by the subject?
> - The indirect object (in Arabic) always follows prepositions.
> - The adverb (of time) answers the "when?" question: When did it happen?

Exercises

EXERCISE 8. Mark all the case endings.

١) وجدتُ السيارة الجديدة أمام البيت القديم.
٢) يزور كل أفراد العائلة هذه المنطقة الجميلة.
٣) ينتهى بناء المكتبة الجديدة في منتصف الشهر المقبل.
٤) تختلف اللغة العربية الفصحى عن اللغة العامية في بعض الكلمات والقواعد.
٥) تعرّف الشاب السعودي على أصحابه الجُدُد.
٦) صحا محمد يوم الجمعة في الساعة العاشرة صباحاً.
٧) استعدوا للانتقال إلى شقة جديدة.
٨) اشترتْ كتبا كثيرة من زميلها العربي.
٩) اشترى الولد الصغير الكتاب الصغير.

EXERCISE 9. Spot the mistakes and check the case endings in this text. Mark those that are correct and change those that are incorrect.

جامعتي

جامعتي حديثةٌ وكبيرةٌ ويدرس فيها طلابٌ من أمريكا والكثيرِ من الطلابِ الأجانبَ ومن بينهم طلابُ عربُ. وأعرف الكثيرَ من هؤلاء الطلابِ العربِ. أنا طالبٌ في كليةٍ الطبِ. هذه الكليةُ كبيرةٌ جداً.
تتكون الجامعةُ من الاقسامِ العلميةِ مثل كلياتُ الفيزياءُ والكيمياءُ والزراعةِ. أما من الأقسامِ الأدبيةِ فتجد كليةُ اللغاتُ أضافة إلى كلياتِ التربيةُ والحقوقَ والاقتصادِ وعلمِ الاجتماعُ.

وتدرس صديقتي في معهدٍ الدراساتِ الاسلاميةِ وتخصصَها هو اللغةُ العربيةُ
وآدابُها. سوف أعمل بعد الدراسةُ طبيباً في هذه المدينةِ. أما صديقتي فستسافر
إلى السعوديةِ لمدةٍ سنةٍ في العامِ القادمُ وستكتب رسالتُها للحصولَ على
الدكتوراهُ.

EXERCISE 10. Add the correct case marker between the noun and the suffix.

١) قرأت مقالته.

٢) مقالته جيدة جدا.

٣) وجدت بعض الأخطاء في مقالته.

٤) هذه هي مقالته الأولى.

٥) كتابة مقالته الثانية تحتاج إلى وقت طويل.

٦) سيكتب مقالاته الجديدة في الصيف.

٧) تُرسَل مقالاته إلى المجلات والجرائد.

6 Verbs
الأفعال

1 Personal pronouns الضمائر	78
2 Conjugations تصريف الفعل	78
2.1 Past tense الماضي	78
2.2 Present tense المضارع	79
2.3 Future tense المستقبل	79
3 The famous ten forms of the Arabic verb أوزان الأفعال	81
4 Hollow, defective, irregular or weak verbs الفعل الضعيف أو الشاذ	83
4.1 Quadrilateral verbs	85
5 The dual of verbs المثنى في الفعل	85
6 Object pronouns ضمائر النصب	86
7 The moods of Arabic verbs: المرفوع والمجرور والمنصوب	88
8 Imperatives الأمر	89
9 Negations النفي	90
9.1 ليس	90
10 The voice in Arabic: active and passive صيغة المجهول والمعلوم	93

78 *Speed Up Your Arabic*

A good indicator of jumping to intermediate level on the proficiency scale is a solid command of verbs in the different tenses. However, even at this level students often forget or confuse conjugation patterns and tense markers. They also frequently use the wrong word to negate the verb in the different tenses.

An Arabic verb usually consists of three (rarely four) root letters for the general meaning and several short vowels and affixes to mark the grammatical person or the tense. The Arabic verb has two basic tenses: past and present; three moods, and recognizes gender, number, and voice (active or passive).

1 Personal pronouns الضمائر

It seems odd to start explaining the Arabic verb with an introduction to the pronouns; however, grammatical persons and conjugation of verbs according to them are vital to your proficiency. The Arabic verb can be conjugated according to 12 personal or independent pronouns. English has only nine including the neuter pronoun "it". The neuter pronoun "it" does not exist in Arabic, because an Arabic noun is either masculine or feminine. However, in Arabic only *eight* are used frequently in daily speech. The dual and feminine plural pronouns are also rarely used.

هُنَّ	هُم	أنتُنَّ	أنتُم	نَحنُ	هُما	هي	هو	أنتُما	أنتِ	أنتَ	أنا
they (fem.)	they (masc.)	you (fem.)	you (masc.)	we	the two	she	he	you two	you (fem.)	you (masc.)	I

In most cases, the personal pronoun is omitted because the conjugated verb expresses the grammatical person through prefixes and suffixes. Only if you want to emphasize or highlight the person would you add the pronoun to the verb.

2 Conjugations تصريف الفعل

In order to explain the grammatical functions of the Arabic verb, three example root letters are used: ف – ع – ل to which the short vowels and affixes are added.

2.1 Past tense الماضي

The conjugation of verbs in the past tense is always associated with adding *suffixes* to the core verb.

هو	فَعَلَ
هي	فَعَلَتْ

Verbs الأفعال 79

أنتِ	فَعَلْتِ
أنتَ	فَعَلْتَ
أنا	فَعَلْتُ
هم	فَعَلُوا
أنتم	فَعَلْتُم
نحن	فَعَلْنا

Note that since Arabic does not have a real infinitive form for citing a verb in a dictionary, the هو form of the past tense is often used instead. Thus, if someone asked you how to say "laughing" or "to laugh" in Arabic, the answer would be ضَحِكَ (lit. "he laughed"). The importance of the هو form is shown by its first place in the conjugation chart.

Also compare the spelling of the singular forms (except for هو), which are identical in unvocalized texts. You must refer to the context to determine which form is used.

2.2 Present tense المضارع

The present tense is usually indicated by *prefixes*, with some *suffixes* in the plural forms.

هو	يَفْعَلُ
هي	تَفْعَلُ
أنتَ	تَفْعَلُ
أنتِ	تَفْعَلِينَ
أنا	أفْعَلُ
هم	يَفْعَلُونَ
أنتم	تَفْعَلُونَ
نحن	نَفْعَلُ

Note that in unvocalized texts the أنتَ and هي forms are identical. The context dictates which form is used.

2.3 Future tense المستقبل

Expressing an action in the future tense only requires an additional *prefix* to the present tense form: سَ. Occasionally, and more so in Classical Arabic, a different prefix سوف is found.

سَيَفْعَلُ، سَيَفْعَلُونَ، سَوْفَ يَفْعَلُ، سَوْفَ يَفْعَلُونَ

Exercises

EXERCISE 1. Determine the tense of the verbs in the following sentences.

الزمن	الجملة
ــــ	سافرت خالتي لزيارة العائلة أمس.
ــــ	أدرس اللغة العربية منذ سنتين.
ــــ	بعد الوصول إلى المطار استأجرنا سيارة.
ــــ	اللاعب المشهور زين الدين زيدان سجل ثلاثة أهداف.
ــــ	لم يفهموه.
ــــ	ستبدأ الاجازة بعد أسبوع.
ــــ	في هذه المدينة عمارات عالية تتكون من عشرة طوابق أو أكثر.
ــــ	تتأخر مغادرة الطائرة بنصف ساعة.
ــــ	لن أنساك أبداً.
ــــ	قبل دخول البيت يدق الجرس.

EXERCISE 2. Change the verb from past tense to present tense and vice versa.

المضارع	الماضي
ــــــــــ	لعبنا كرة القدم
أستقبل بالضيوف في المطار.	ــــــــــ
ــــــــــ	جلستُ مع صاحبتي في المقهى.
بعد أسبوعين نسافر إلى بغداد.	ــــــــــ
ــــــــــ	شربتم الشاي بعد الأكل.
تتكلمين مع المدير.	ــــــــــ
ــــــــــ	رجعتْ البنت من الرحلة.
ينعقد المؤتمر في الرياض.	ــــــــــ
ــــــــــ	دخّنوا خارج المطعم.
ترجعون إلى البيت متأخرين.	ــــــــــ
ــــــــــ	شاهدتَ الفيديو.
يأكلون طعام العشاء.	ــــــــــ
ــــــــــ	دخل الغرفة.

81 الأفعال / Verbs

المضارع	الماضي
تدرس اللغة العربية.	_____
_____	قرأتِ الجريدة.
تذهب الموظفة إلى المكتب.	_____

3 The famous ten forms of the Arabic verb أوزان الأفعال

While the three root letters only give the general meaning of the word, the specific verb needs an arrangement or pattern, in Arabic وَزْن ج أوْزان, of short vowels and affixes to create a real word. It is possible and common to have more than one verb of the same root. However, they will differ in their pattern. Arabic knows 15 verb patterns, but only ten are used frequently.

Examples:

دَرَسَ – دَرَّسَ – دارَسَ – أَدْرَسَ
عَرِفَ – عَرَّفَ – تَعَرَّفَ – اِعْتَرَفَ
قَطَعَ – قَطَّعَ – قاطَعَ – أَقْطَعَ – تَقَطَّعَ – تَقاطَعَ – اِنْقَطَعَ – اِقْتَطَعَ – اِسْتَقْطَعَ

Tip
How can we determine which the correct form is? In order to use the forms efficiently, you first must determine which letter is part of the root and which letter is part of the pattern. The last letter of the verb (of course in the هو form) is always the third root letter. And the second to last letter is the second root letter. Now remember they might be vowels! The first root letter is more difficult to find. But as a rule of thumb, letters like ت, م, س and ن are more likely to be part of the pattern than part of the root. If the verb is not vocalized that makes it even harder and you have to check several possibilities. A good friend and helper is Hans Wehr's Arabic–English dictionary, which is organized according to the root letters and lists the existing forms for each verb. A Roman number is given to each form, which helps you to recognize the pattern. But even then it is difficult for verbs like اِنْتَقَلَ, which can be VII or VIII. But remember that VII is a very rare pattern or a passive voice. So, in most cases you are fine with VIII.

It is extremely helpful to memorize the following chart. I recommend that you memorize it with familiar, frequently used verbs. Here are my favorites:

	الوزن	الماضي	المضارع	المصدر	الترجمة
I	فَعَلَ	كَتَبَ	يَكْتُبُ	الكِتَابَة	to write
II	فَعَّلَ	دَخَّنَ	يُدَخِّنُ	التَدْخِين	to smoke
III	فَاعَلَ	سَاعَدَ	يُسَاعِدُ	المُسَاعَدَة	to help
IV	أَفْعَلَ	أَرَادَ	يُرِيدُ	الإِرَادَة	to want
V	تَفَعَّلَ	تَكَلَّمَ	يَتَكَلَّمُ	التَكَلُّم	to talk
VI	تَفَاعَلَ	تَبَادَلَ	يَتبَادَلُ	التَبَادُل	to exchange
VII	اِنْفَعَلَ	اِنْقَطَعَ	يَنْقَطِعُ	الاِنْقِطاع	to cut
VIII	اِفْتَعَلَ	اِجْتَمَعَ	يَجْتَمِعُ	الاِجْتِماع	to meet
IX	اِفْعَلَّ	اِحْمَرَّ	يَحْمَرُّ	الاِحْمِرار	to turn red
X	اِسْتَفْعَلَ	اِسْتَمْتَعَ	يَسْتَمْتِعُ	الاِسْتِمْتاع	to enjoy

The first pattern, although one of the most common, is somewhat different because it actually includes three forms of الماضي and three related forms of المضارع. In addition, the مصدر varies from form to form and is thus very unpredictable.

	الوزن	الماضي	المضارع	المصدر	الترجمة
I	فَعَلَ – يَفْعُلُ	كَتَبَ	يَكْتُبُ	الكِتابة	to write
I	فَعَلَ – يَفْعِلُ	عَقَدَ	يَعْقِدُ	العَقْد	to gather
I	فَعِلَ – يَفْعَلُ	شَرِبَ	يَشْرَبُ	الشُرْب	to drink

Note that the verbal noun, or المصدر, represents the gerund form or infinitive. I added the article to remind you that the مصدر is a noun, not a verb.

> **Tip**
> I highly recommended that you memorize these three forms of each new verb: الماضي – المضارع – المصدر. This allows you to conjugate it in all directions and to use the word in different tenses and in many contexts.

Exercise

EXERCISE 3. Fill in the blanks.

الوزن	الماضي	المضارع	المصدر	الترجمة
___	___	___	التعامل	___
___	___	يشترك	___	___
___	أرسل	___	___	___
___	___	يتفرج	___	___
___	___	___	التحقيق	___
___	شاهد	___	___	___
___	___	___	القراءة	___
___	استثمر	___	___	___
___	___	ينعقد	___	___

4 Hollow, defective, irregular or weak verbs الفعل الضعيف أو الشاذ

Whatever you like to call them, some verbs have a different format based on their root, which may contain special letters like hamza, long vowels or shaddas. Some verbs even contain two special root letters. This often leads to modified conjugations, which is shown in a different spelling and pronunciation. As a rule of thumb, it is helpful to first recognize the weak verb, then find a example verb that you often use and then memorize its conjugation. In order to identify the three root letters, you should look at the ten forms, both the past and the present. As always, memorize the third person singular past and present and use it as a starter to derive the other forms and grammatical persons.

Common weak verbs include:

الترجمة	المصدر	المضارع	الماضي	Special feature
to arrive	الوُصول	يَصِلُ	وَصَلَ	First root letter is a vowel.
to be	الكَوْن	يكونُ	كانَ	Second root letter is a vowel.
to walk	المشى	يَمْشي	مَشى	Third root letter is a vowel.
to eat	الأكل	يأكُلُ	أكَلَ	First root letter is hamza.

84 *Speed Up Your Arabic*

Special feature	الماضي	المضارع	المصدر	الترجمة
Second and third root letters are identical.	رَدَّ	يَرُدُّ	الرَّدّ	to repeat
Second and third root letters are vowels.	نَوَى	يَنْوِي	النِّية	to intend
VIII form, third root letter is a vowel.	اِنْتَهَى	يَنْتَهِي	الإِنْتِهَاء	to finish
VIII form, third root letter is a vowel.	اِشْتَرَى	يَشْتَرِي	الشِّرَاء	to buy
Second root letter is a vowel.	بَاعَ	يَبِيعُ	البِيع	to sell
Second root letter is hamza.	سَأَلَ	يَسْأَلُ	السُّؤال	to ask
X form, first root letter is hamza.	اِسْتَأْجَرَ	يَسْتَأْجِرُ	الإِسْتِئْجَار	to rent

Note that weak verbs occur in many of the derived forms too.

Exercises

EXERCISE 4. Check the use of the weak verb in the following sentences and mark if it is correct or not.

صواب أو خطأ	الفعل الضعيف
_____	خافتْ البنت من العاصفة.
_____	باعنا بيتنا.
_____	نشترى الخضار من السوق.
_____	سألته عن القضية.
_____	أأكل العشاء في المطعم.
_____	مشتُ ساعات طويلة.
_____	كانا أنا وأصحابي سعداء.
_____	يصلون إلى المطار.
_____	تنتهي المباراة في الساعة الخامسة.
_____	هل أرادتم الخروج؟

EXERCISE 5. Change the conjugation from the third person singular past tense to the first person singular past tense.

الفعل الضعيف الماضي – أنا	الفعل الضعيف الماضي – هو/هي
_____	زار الرئيس المنطقة الشمالية.
_____	عادت من النادي متأخرة.
_____	كان جوعان جدا.

Verbs الأفعال 85

الفعل الضعيف الماضي – أنا	الفعل الضعيف الماضي – هو/هي
_____	قالت له إنها مرتاحة.
_____	انتهى من الواجبات.
_____	باعت ملابس شتوية.
_____	وصل صديقي مساء الأمس.
_____	تمنى أن يكون مثلها.
_____	اشترى تذكرتين للمباراة.
_____	أرادت البقاء في البيت.
_____	أعطته المفتاح.

4.1 Quadrilateral verbs

There is only a handful of verbs that have four root letters. Just be aware of this and look them up in a dictionary when you come across them. At times, they are called form XI. Here are some examples:

to translate	ترجم – يترجم	to rule	سيطر – يسيطر
to link together	سلسل – يسلسل	to rattle	خشخش – يخشخش
to chat	دردش – يدردش	to call/phone	تلفن – يتلفن

5 The dual of verbs المثنى في الفعل

The two-form in Arabic is marked on nouns, adjectives, and pronouns as well as on verbs. However, in the past tense only the هو, هي and أنتم pronouns take the dual suffix ا. In the present tense the suffix is انِ and is attached to the هو, هي and أنتَ forms. They represent the dual personal pronouns of هما and أنتما (see the chart of personal pronouns above). In colloquial Arabic most dual endings on verbs are omitted; they are only mentioned here for your information. You should, however, be aware of the concept, especially since this is one of the rare forms where an Arabic word ends with the letter ا.

Examples:

الترجمة	المضارع	الترجمة	الماضي	الضمير
the two (masc.) travel	يُسَافِرَانِ	the two (masc.) traveled	سَافَرَا	هما
the two (fem.) travel	تُسَافِرَانِ	the two (fem.) traveled	سَافَرَتَا	هما
you two travel	تُسَافِرَانِ	you two traveled	سَافَرْتُمَا	أنتما

86 *Speed Up Your Arabic*

Exercise

EXERCISE 6. Add the correct form of the verb.

١) الوالدان _____ (يسكن) في نفس البيت.

٢) أنا وأخي _____ (سافر) لزيارة جدنا أمس.

٣) الرئيسان السوري والايراني _____ (يناقش) قضايا مهمة في زيارة عمل.

٤) علمتُ بأن أخي خالد وصديقتي مريم _____ (تزوج) قبل أسبوع.

٥) الفريقان الأهلي والشباب _____ (يشارك) في بطولة كأس الأبطال.

٦) يا سليمان وعلي، هل _____ (ساعد) عم حسين في شغل المحل؟

٧) غدا، أنتما _____ (يزور) الجيران.

٨) الطالبتان _____ (نجح) في التوجيهي.

6 Object pronouns ضمائر النصب

As we have learned, Arabic has three distinct types of pronouns: personal, object and possessive pronouns. Only the first two affect the verb. Object pronouns are attached to verbs and express meanings such as "I love *him*" or "they helped *me*". Just as English object pronouns differ from personal pronouns (me – I, him – he), so do Arabic object pronouns. Students often forget, however, that the latter are attached to the verb and are not individual words.

Examples:

صواب	خطأ
أنا أساعدك	أنا أساعد أنت
أنت تحبني	أنت تحب أنا
حصلنا عليه	حصلنا على هو

The only difference between object pronouns and possessive pronouns is the additional letter نـ in the first form (me vs. my): تفهمني – كتابي (my book – you understand me).

الأفعال Verbs

> **Mnemonic device**
> The following invented phrase summarizes the use of the object pronouns:
>
> You asked me it.   سألتمونيها
>
> In this phrase you find a past tense verb with two object pronouns all linked together. Please note the added letter و, which serves as a connector between two syllables that would not otherwise connect.

Exercises

EXERCISE 7. Translate and add the correct object pronoun.

I love you.   _____
He hates me.   _____
Can you help me please?   _____
They don't understand us.   _____
She took it from me.   _____
He left her and her family.   _____
This suits me very well.   _____
I bought it for only 10 riyal.   _____
Please give me your phone number.   _____
He saw her last night.   _____

EXERCISE 8. Decide which phrase contains an object pronoun (النصب) and which has a possessive pronoun (الملك).

ضمير الملك أو النصب؟	الجملة بالضمير
_____	يعيش مع أسرته.
_____	يساعد أخته بالواجب.
_____	يساعدها كثيرا.
_____	لا يحبونه.
_____	قابلتهم في المدينة.
_____	استقبلني في المطار.
_____	خذ راحتك.
_____	أريد مساعدتكم.
_____	هل يمكنكم أن تساعدوني؟
_____	اشتريته من السوق.

7 The moods of Arabic verbs:
المرفوع والمجرور والمنصوب

Here is another case of special verbal forms which are common in MSA, but rarely used in colloquial Arabic. Even so-called "educated" Arabic, which calls for a balance of both vernaculars, often omits these endings. Mood indicates the speaker's attitude towards a subject. While English has three moods, Arabic knows four: المرفوع, المنصوب, المجزوم and الأمر. المرفوع, the indicative mood, describes the actual, real state of something; المنصوب or the subjunctive mood deals with states of unreality; and المجزوم or the jussive is used for commanding and exhorting. Finally, الأمر is the imperative mood or command form. In Arabic these moods are derived from the present tense and marked with a specific short vowel. المرفوع takes **-u**, المنصوب takes **-a** and المجزوم takes no short vowel (sukuun). المرفوع is the most common form, almost like the default form. المنصوب and المجزوم occur only after special words or particles.

Used after	Short vowel marker	Mood
	ُ	مرفوع
أنْ، لَنْ، لِ، لكي، حتى	َ	منصوب
لَمْ، لِ	ْ	مجزوم

Tip
You can replace أنْ + منصوب with the المصدر:

يحبون أنْ يقرأوا الجرائد. ← يحبون قراءة الجرائد.

Exercise

EXERCISE 9. Replace the أنْ phrase with the مصدر and vice versa.

أنا آسف ولكني لا أستطيع أنْ أخرجَ معكم. _____

_____ شجعني والدي على الالتحاق بالجيش.

يمكنك أنْ تدفعَ الحساب غدا. _____

_____ قررنا البقاء في هذه المنطقة.

أتمنى أن أنتقل إلى مدينة بعيدة. _____

_____ أراد الشعب إرحال الرئيس الظالم.

Verbs الأفعال 89

إسمح لي أن أقدمَ نفسي.

طلبتُ منهم العودة إلى البيت فوراً. _____

يجب عليّ أنْ أدرسَ وأحفظَ كثيراً
قبل أنْ أتخرجَ من الجامعة. _____

When do we need to use these moods? The most obvious case is when you attach an object pronoun to the verb, for example when you want to say "I love you" or "Can you help us?". Note that in the second example the connecting vowel between the two verbs and pronouns is different.

أُحِبُّكِ   هل يمكنُك أن تساعدَنا؟

You might say these are nuances, but they are important, especially when it comes to imperatives.

8 Imperatives الأمر

In order to give commands, both positive and negative, a special pattern of vocalizing the Arabic verb is used. Of course, this pattern is different from form to form with Form I being the most frequently used. In Form I, you start with the هو form present tense and drop the conjugation marker. Then you replace it with alif hamza. Note that this hamza is vocalized with either **-i** (إذْهَبْ) or **-u** (أُدْخُلْ), depending on the short vowel after the second root letter (see the present tense conjugation for Form I in section 2.2 above). For plural commands the syllable وا is added and when talking to females you add ي. The other forms are regular derivatives from the present tense form:

الترجمة	الأمر	الفعل المضارع	الوزن
Watch!	فَرِّجْ / فَرِّجوا	يُفَرِّجُ	II
Help!	ساعِدْ / ساعِدوا	يُساعِدُ	III
Close!	إغْلَقْ / إغْلَقوا	يُغْلِقُ	IV
Talk!	تَكَلَّمْ / تَكَلَّمُوا	يَتَكَلَّمُ	V
Get to know each other!	تَعَارَفْ / تَعَارَفُوا	يَتَعَارَفُ	VI
Withdraw!	إنْصَرِفْ / إنْصَرِفوا	يَنْصَرِفُ	VII
Smile!	ابْتَسِمْ / ابْتَسِموا	يَبْتَسِمُ	VIII
Enjoy!	إسْتَمْتِعْ / إسْتَمْتِعُوا	يَسْتَمْتِعُ	X

Exercise

EXERCISE 10. Give the correct command.

Get up!	يقوم	_____
Eat!	يأكل	_____
Sit!	يجلس	_____
Ask!	يسأل	_____
Write!	يكتب	_____
Come back!	يرجع	_____
Be quiet!	يسكت	_____
Watch!	يشاهد	_____
Play!	يلعب	_____
Grab!	يمسك	_____

9 Negations النفي

Each tense and mood has its own negator:

Negating the present tense	لا + المرفوع
Negating the imperative	لا + الجزوم
Negating the past tense (formal)	لم + الجزوم
Negating the future tense	لن + المنصوب
Negating the past tense	ما + الماضي
Negating "to have" and "to be" (present tense only)	ليس

9.1 ليس

Negating a sentence with a verb is simple; just remember to use the correct negator. However, it is often confusing for students to negate sentences that do not include a verb, those nominal sentences that express "to be" and "to have". In MSA the word ليس is used for this purpose, although only in the present tense when you want to say "I am not hungry" or "the car is not expensive" or "she doesn't have classes".

Verbs الأفعال 91

Negating "to be"

ليس is used to negate "to be" in the present tense: "I am not, you are not, he is not, ...". The odd thing is the fact that ليس is conjugated like a past tense verb. Essentially, a past tense verb is used to negate the present tense of "to be". For the past tense of "to be" ("I was, you were", etc.) the regular negation rules apply.

Examples:

I am not hungry.	لَسْتُ جوعاناً.
The car is not expensive.	ليست السيارة غالية.
There is no choice.	ليس هناك خيار.
They are not from here.	لَيْسوا من هنا.
We are not OK.	لسنا بخير.
I was not hungry.	ما كُنْتُ جوعاناً / لم أكُنْ جوعاناً.

Negating "to have"

In Arabic "to have" is not expressed by a regular verb, but by a prepositional phrase. In order to negate "to have" in the present tense ليس is placed in front of the preposition. However, unlike in the previous case, ليس is not conjugated. The past tense negation uses the regular negators. Note that in colloquial Arabic this type of ليس is replaced by ما.

Examples:

I don't have a brother.	ليس لي أخ.
She doesn't have a large house.	ليس عندها بيت كبير.
This city doesn't have a university.	هذه المدينة ليس فيها جامعة.
They don't have time today.	ليس لهم وقت اليوم.
We don't have a problem.	ليس عندنا مشكلة.

This form is also used to negate common impersonal phrases like "It is necessary to" or "It is strange that".

Examples:

It is/it isn't necessary to ...	ليس من الضروري أن	من الضروري أن
It is/it isn't strange that ...	ليس من الغريب أن	من الغريب أن
It is/it isn't hard to ...	ليس من الصعب أن	من الصعب أن

Exercises

EXERCISE 11. Negate the following questions and statements.

هو رجل طويل. _____
نريد أن نزور الأردن في الصيف. _____
أغضب منك. _____
اليوم عندنا واجبات كثيرة. _____
كان الامتحان صعب جدا. _____
هل فهمتم هذا السؤال؟ _____
يشترك كل الطلاب في مباراة كرة القدم. _____
يملك الناس في مصر الحرية. _____
هل يمكنني أن أخرج مع أصدقائي في الليل؟ _____
سأتخرج من الجامعة بعد هذا الفصل. _____
هل عندك وقت بعد الظهر؟ _____
كانت البنت مشغولة بواجباتها. _____
في هذه المدينة شوارع كثيرة. _____

EXERCISE 12. Negate the following imperatives.

إقرأ الجملة! _____
خذي الشنطة! _____
أدخلوا الغرفة! _____
إمش إلى هناك! _____
أكتب لي! _____
إشربي القهوة! _____
كرروا الكلمات! _____
أمسك الصورة! _____
إذهب إلى هذا المكان! _____
سافروا معهم! _____

10 The voice in Arabic: active and passive صيغة المجهول والمعلوم

Verbal voice in Arabic does not relate to the next Arab superstar, but to the expression of active or passive statements, for example, "he writes" versus "something was written". In Arabic this is shown by using a different vocalization. Please note that the spelling of the verb usually does not change. In unvocalized texts, the active and passive voices are often identical and the context allows the reader to recognize the difference. The active voice is vocalized كَتَبَ - يَكْتُبُ and the passive voice is كُتِبَ - يُكْتَبُ. Again, this applies to all derived forms.

But don't panic! It happens to the best not to recognize the passive voice when reading an unfamiliar text. They simply start again and read it correctly. A few verbs are more often used in the passive voice and I recommend that you memorize them.

يوجَدُ، وُلِدَ، يُعْتَبَرُ، يُسَمَّى، يُحْتَمَلُ

> **Tip**
> Arabic offers a way of describing the passive voice. Use يَتِمُّ - تَمَّ or المصدر + يَجْري - جَرَى instead of the often complicated passive voice.

Note that we can only derive the passive voice from transitive verbs, i.e. those verbs that take a direct object.

Exercises

EXERCISE 13. Change the following sentences from the active to the passive voice.

أقام الوزير حفلة عشاء.	أُقيمتْ حفلة عشاء.
غيّر الرئيس البرنامج.	_____
شاهدنا الطلاب أمام الجامعة.	_____
يسلّم أحمد الكتاب غداً.	_____
كتب الكاتب الكتاب.	_____
منع الوالد التدخين.	_____
يعتبر الطلاب الدرس سهلاً.	_____
طبخت الوالدة الطعام للإفطار.	_____

94 *Speed Up Your Arabic*

EXERCISE 14. Mark the verbs (29) in the following text and describe their tense, person and pattern under the headings given below, then translate the text.

في الأسبوع الماضي قابلت صديقي رضوان الذي يسكن في سوريا ولكن جاء لزيارتي. ذهبنا أنا وهو إلى مطعم صغير للعشاء حيث أكل رضوان كباب وأكلت أنا شوربة وسلطة. ما كان الأكل لذيذ. بعد الأكل شربنا الشاي ودخنا سيجارة. استمعنا إلى الأخبار وتكلمت المذيعة عن الحرب في سوريا. أخيرا جاء الوقت للكلام عما حدث هناك في الشهور الماضية. شرح لي بأن أسرته فرضت عليها الهروب من القرية. ما زالوا يعيشون في مخيم اللاجئين. ولكن سافر هو وأخته إلى لبنان حيث لقينا من جديد. اليوم سأرجع إلى شقته التي استأجرها منذ أسبوع مرة أخرى لأننا يجب علينا أن نحكي عن أشياء كثيرة. سمعت أنه وجد وظيفة جديدة. أما اخته التي حصلت على البكالوريوس في التعليم فتبحث عن وظيفة أيضاً. أريد أن أساعدها في هذا البحث.

الوزن	الشخص	الزمن	الفعل
_____	_____	_____	_____
_____	_____	_____	_____
_____	_____	_____	_____
_____	_____	_____	_____
_____	_____	_____	_____
_____	_____	_____	_____
_____	_____	_____	_____
_____	_____	_____	_____
_____	_____	_____	_____
_____	_____	_____	_____
_____	_____	_____	_____
_____	_____	_____	_____
_____	_____	_____	_____
_____	_____	_____	_____

7 Word order and sentence structure
تركيب الجمل

1 Nominal sentences الجملة الاسمية 96
2 Verbal sentences الجملة الفعلية 98
3 Adverbial time clauses 100
4 Causal sentences 102
5 Conditional sentences جملة الشرط 104
6 Relative sentences جملة الصفة والصلة 105
7 Exception clauses جملة الاستثناء 108
8 Circumstantial clauses جملة الحال 109
9 Questions السؤال 111

SENTENCE STRUCTURE IS DIFFERENT IN ARABIC

For the non-native speaker word order and structure of the Arabic sentence often seem confusing because they follow a format different from English syntax. Although the components of the sentence, such as subject, object and verb, are the same as in English, they are arranged in a different order, which requires you to revise your habitual practices. It is strange to say the verb before the subject, but you have to remind yourself to do this again and again! As a rule of thumb the information that is already known and is thus definite comes first, and the stuff that is new and is indefinite comes last. When both parts are known or new, then the subject comes before the object. The verb–subject–object word order is more common in MSA, while colloquial Arabic frequently sees subject–verb–object.

Tip
Don't trust Arabic punctuation marks. The English system of separating clauses or phrases by periods, commas or semicolons is not applicable to Arabic. Instead other markers and conjunctions are used.

Arabic recognizes two common types of sentence, the nominal and the verbal sentence. The nominal sentence starts with a noun (or pronoun) and the verbal sentence with a verb. Simplified word order in the nominal sentence is S–V–O (subject–verb–object) and V–S–O (verb–subject–object) in the verbal sentence.

1 Nominal sentences الجملة الاسمية

The nominal sentence contains two parts, the subject المبتدأ and the predicate الخبر. This sentence begins with the subject, as we are used to in English. The subject is either a noun or a pronoun. The second part of the sentence, the predicate, can be either an adjective, a noun, a prepositional phrase or a verb.

Examples:

The car is expensive.	السيارة غالية.
The girl is a student.	البنت طالبة.
She is in school.	هي في المدرسة.
You are hungry.	أنت جوعان.
My grandfather is Iraqi.	جدي عراقي.
This is an old house.	هذا بيت قديم.

الطالبة تدرس.	The student studies.
الوالدان يسكنان في هذه القرية.	The parents live in this village.
في هذه المنطقة مدارس جيدة.	Good schools are in this area.
عندي سيارة جديدة.	I have a new car.

Note that in the last two examples the subject is not at the beginning of the sentence but at the end. The reason is that nominal sentences cannot begin with an indefinite noun. In this case the word order must be reversed: first comes the predicate, and then comes the subject.

You may also note that the nominal sentence does not need to have a verb. This makes the nominal sentence look very odd because as English speakers we are used to seeing a verb in every sentence. The type of nominal sentence that does not include a verb is called an equational sentence.

Tip
The two important verbs "to be" and "to have" are not expressed as verbal sentences; instead their meaning is implied and expressed in a nominal/equational sentence or the meaning is expressed through a prepositional phrase.

It has already been mentioned that there has to be agreement between the subject and predicate in gender and number. See Chapter 4.

Exercise

EXERCISE 1. Translate the following nominal sentences.

الوضع الاقتصادي في أوروبا صعب.
_____

_____
My family is very poor.

هم يسكنون جنب المسجد.
_____

_____
I have only one sister.

الأكل اللبناني لذيذ جداً.
_____

_____
Today the weather is sunny and warm.

لها بنت في الروضة.
_____

_____
Do you have any time this afternoon?

98 *Speed Up Your Arabic*

هل عندك كمبيوتر في البيت؟

_____

The post office is near the train station. _____

في المنزل ثلاثة طوابق.

_____

My friends are from Sudan. _____

الرئيس الجديد غير محبوب لدى الجماهير.

_____

Do you have a question? _____

الجو في الجبال بارد في الشتاء.

_____

Cairo is an old and beautiful city. _____

هي مريضة.

_____

We have a farm in the countryside. _____

والدي يعمل في التجارة.

_____

Studying Arabic is hard! _____

2 Verbal sentences الجملة الفعلية

The first word in a verbal sentence is a verb. Often the subject is included (and expressed by the conjugation, see Chapter 6, section 2). Then, theoretically, the sentence may consist of one word only. If there is a separate subject it follows the verb. However, in this case a different agreement rule applies: if the verb precedes the subject, then it is used in the singular form only. The gender agreement remains.

Examples:

He studies.	يدرس.
He studies at the university.	يدرس في الجامعة.
The (male) student studies at the university.	يدرس الطالب في الجامعة.
The (female) student studies at the university.	تدرس الطالبة في الجامعة.
The (male) students study at the university.	يدرس الطلاب في الجامعة.
The (female) students study at the university.	تدرس الطالبات في الجامعة.
The lessons are studied at the university.	تُدرس الدروس في الجامعة.

Word order and sentence structure تركيب الجمل 99

The last example is there to remind you that the plurals of things and non-humans are treated like feminine singulars!

Both verbal and nominal sentences are interchangeable and used frequently. But how can we differentiate between them, and how do we know which one to use?

Most things can be said in either way. To simplify the matter, we can say that colloquial Arabic tends to use nominal sentences more often, while formal Arabic, especially media Arabic, prefers the verbal sentence. In many instances, the context dictates which sentence must be used. If it does not include a verb, use the nominal sentence and if it does, choose the verbal sentence. However, the following conjunction requires a nominal sentence (even if it includes a verb). After أنّ you must use a noun or pronoun (see Chapter 9, section 8).

Examples:

أظن أنّ الطالب يدرس في هذه الجامعة.
أظن أنه يدرس هناك.

Exercises

EXERCISE 2. Unscramble the words in the following sentences and put them in the right order.

موظف شركة في والدي آرامكو السعودية في. _____
كل ساعات يعمل يوم طويلة. _____
وقت عائلة ليس مع لديه. _____
للسباحة كلنا نذهب البحر إلى. _____
الكُرة يلعب إخوتي وأخواتي مع. _____
غروب البيت نعود إلى الشمس بعد. _____
الدوام في الشركة في يبدأ الصباح غدا. _____
المدرسة الأولاد يدرس في. _____

100 *Speed Up Your Arabic*

EXERCISE 3. Transform the verbal sentences into nominal sentences and vice versa.

الجملة الفعلية	الجملة الاسمية
ــــــــــــــــــــــــــــ	الطالبات تشربن الشاي بعد المحاضرات.
التحق الشباب بالجيش.	ــــــــــــــــــــــــــــ
ــــــــــــــــــــــــــــ	قوات الاحتلال ترفع حصارها على الأقصى
تطور شركة كانون عدسة سينمائية جديدة.	ــــــــــــــــــــــــــــ
تعادل إنتر وميونخ في كأس الأبطال.	الفُرق العربية تودع أبطال آسيا
ــــــــــــــــــــــــــــ	المشاكل المالية تقلل القدرة على التفكير.
شاركت جميع أندية الطلبة في مهرجان الجامعة.	ــــــــــــــــــــــــــــ
ــــــــــــــــــــــــــــ	نواب مجلس الشورى عقدوا اجتماعا.
لم يسافر الأولاد مع والديهم.	الطلاب استمعوا إلى محاضرة الأستاذ.
ــــــــــــــــــــــــــــ	ــــــــــــــــــــــــــــ
توفر الجامعات الأوربية منحا للطلاب الأجانب.	العثمانيون انسحبوا من بغداد عام ١٩١٧.
يتغيب طلاب كثيرون عن دراساتهم بسبب الجو المثلج.	ــــــــــــــــــــــــــــ
ــــــــــــــــــــــــــــ	القوات السورية تستخدم سلاح الحرمان من الصحة.
اكتمل بناء جامع القرويين في مدينة فاس عام ٨٥٩.	ــــــــــــــــــــــــــــ

3 Adverbial time clauses

Time clauses are used with subordinate clauses. They show that the action of the subordinate clause happened before, during or after the action of the main clause. For each time frame a special conjunction is used to introduce the time clause. The most common conjunctions are:

Word order and sentence structure تركيب الجمل 101

منذ	حتى	قبل أنْ	بعد أنْ	بينما	لما	عندما
since	until	before	after	while	when (dialect)	when (MSA)

Examples:

Simultaneity

I forgot the key when I left home.

نسيتُ المفتاح عندما تركتُ المنزل.

I will give you the book when I finish reading it.

سأعطيك الكتاب عندما أنتهي من قراءته.

When I was in Saudi Arabia I lived in a big house.

عندما كنتُ في السعودية سكنت في بيت كبير.

The student commits mistakes when he learns Arabic.

يرتكب الطالب أخطأ بينما يدرس اللغة العربية.

When I came to visit you, I found the door locked.

لما جئتُ لزيارتك وجدتُ الباب مغلقاً.

After I heard the president's speech I felt angry.

لما سمعت كلام الرئيس كنت أشعر مزعجاً.

She left him while he was asleep.

تركتْه بينما كان نائماً.

Anteriority

I drank tea after I ate dinner.

شربت الشاي بعد أن أكلت العشاء.

Since I graduated from university, I have been working for Aramco.

منذ أن تخرجت من الجامعة أشتغل في شركة آرامكو.

The child cried after his mother left him.

بكى الطفل بعد أن تركته أمه.

After finishing work we take a long break.

بعد إنجاز العمل نأخذ راحة طويلة.

Posteriority

I ask my dad before I go out with my friends.

أسأل والدي قبل أن أخرج مع أصحابي.

Close the door before leaving the house.

إغلق الباب قبل نزول من البيت.

Don't forget your ablutions before you pray.

لا تنسى الوضوء قبل أن تصلي.

He studied for many hours until he memorized all the information.

درس ساعات طويلة حتى حفظ المعلومات كلها.

Exercise

EXERCISE 4. Combine the two clauses with the conjunction عندما or لما to create meaningful clauses of time.

فنح الباب.	عندما رجعتُ إلى المنزل
كنتُ حزيناً وبكيتُ كثيراً.	عندما كنت في القاهرة
تطبخ الزوجة العشاء.	عندما وصلوا إلى المسرح
أصحو متأخراً في الصباح الثاني.	عندما سمعتْ الخبر الأبيض
ذهبوا إلى مقاعدهم على الطول.	عندما سمعتُ خبر وفاة عمي
زرت الأهرام.	عندما يشاهد الزوج التلفزيون
كان العشاء جاهزاً.	عندما أسهر مع الأصحاب
كانت سعيدة جداً.	عندما دق الباب

4 Causal sentences

A causal sentence indicates a reason or answer to the لماذا ("why?") question. The following conjunctions are used to introduce the causal sentence, which is typically a nominal sentence:

لأنَّ، بِسَبَب، لِ، مِن أجْل

Students frequently pick the wrong conjunction when answering the "why?" question. Usually they go with بِسَبَب because it was introduced first and does not require any modification. However, each conjunction requires a particular word or sentence type to follow:

لأنَّ – الجملة الاسمية
بِسَبَب – اسم وإضافة
لِ – فعل في المضارع المنصوب
مِن أجْل – اسم، اضافة، ضمير الملك

Word order and sentence structure تركيب الجمل 103

Before answering the "why?" question, consider the grammatical form you want to use. Perhaps you would like to give a longer answer in the form of a sentence: then you should use لأنَّ. If you only want to give a short, one or two word answer, use بِسَبَب.

Examples:

He did not attend the party because he was sick.
لم يحضر الحفلة لأنَّهُ كان مريضاً.

We memorize these words because they are very useful for conversations.
نحفظ هذه الكلمات والمفردات لأنها مفيدة جداً في المحادثة.

The street is closed because of the heavy snow.
الشارع مغلق بسبب الثلج الشديد.

I love her because she is beautiful and kind.
أحبها لأنها جميلة ولطيفة.

I love her because of her beauty and kindness.
أحبها بسبب جمالها ولطافتها.

We traveled to the capital because of the demonstrations.
سافرنا إلى العاصمة من أجل المظاهرات.

We study foreign languages in order to get good jobs.
ندرس لغة أجنبية لنحصلَ على وظيفة جيدة.

The West steps up against Syria because of the "chemicals".
تصعيد غربي ضد دمشق بسبب "الكيماوي"

He came to Saudi Arabia to look for a job.
جاء إلى السعودية ليبحث عن وظيفة.

I stayed at home because the weather was rainy.
بقيتُ في البيت لأن الطقس كان ممطرا.

Exercise

EXERCISE 5. Choose the correct conjunction to complete the sentences.

١) ألغينا رحلتنا إلى بيروت _____ الأحداث بسوريا.
٢) أحبك _____ أجمل فتاة في العالم.
٣) كل شيء يحدث _____.
٤) ذهبنا إلى الملعب _____ مشاهدة المباراة.

104 Speed Up Your Arabic

٥) أنا زعلان جدا ـــــــــ فريقي خسر هذه المباراة المهمة.

٦) بقيت في البيت ـــــــــ أقضي وقتا طيبا مع عائلتي.

٧) فشل في الامتحان ـــــــــ الأخطاء الكثيرة.

٨) لم يحضر الحفلة ـــــــــ كان مريضاً.

5 Conditional sentences جملة الشرط

These expressions usually include two clauses, the main clause and the conditional clause, following the model: "If . . . , then . . .". Unlike in English, the Arabic conditional clause usually precedes the main clause. Arabic distinguishes between real and unreal conditions. Real conditional sentences are introduced by إذا or إنْ, where إنْ tends to be more formal and certain. Unreal conditions are introduced by لَوْ. Remember to use the past tense after all conjunctions, because there is no tense agreement between the clauses! The second part of the conditional construct may be introduced by a conjunction following the model:

if	then
إذا	ف
لو	لـ

Mnemonic device
These four conjunctions have a nice rhyme and it is worth remembering the simple tune:

idha fa law la, idha fa law la, idha fa law la.

Examples:

If I were a king I would live in a palace.
لو كنتُ ملكاً لَعشتُ في قصر.

If I travel to Saudi Arabia then I will visit my relatives in Riyadh.
إذا سافرتُ إلى السعودية فَسأزور أقاربي في الرياض.

If you agree, we will leave immediately.
إذا كنتَ موافقاً سنغادر فوراً.

If you like this dress then let's buy it.
إذا أعجبك هذا الفستان فَلِنَشْتَره.

Word order and sentence structure تركيب الجمل

If the weather is nice today then we will go to the mountains.
إذا كان الجو جميلاً اليوم فَسَنُسافر إلى الجبال.

If I didn't study Arabic, I wouldn't be able to talk to the Arabs.
لو لم أدرسْ عربي لما استطعْتُ الكلام مع العرب.

If you are a liar, be a smart one.
إن كنتَ كذوبا فكُنْ ذكورا.

When Ahmad comes, I will ask him.
إذا جاء أحمد أسألَهُ.

If you study, you will be successful.
إن تُذاكِر تَنْجَح.

Say hi to him when you meet him.
سلِّمْ لي عليه اذا قابلتَهُ.

Exercise

EXERCISE 6. Complete the following conditional sentences.

١) لو كنتُ مليونيراً
٢) إن كنتَ حبيبي
٣) ماذا تفعلون إذا
٤) إذا لم تحضر غدا
٥) إذا ذهبنا إلى الأردن
٦) لو كان عندي وقت
٧) إذا لم ترجع قبل منتصف الليل
٨) لو تركتُه
٩) لو كان الصيف
١٠) إن تحضر الحفلة

6 Relative sentences جملة الصفة والصلة

A relative clause is used to add information to a noun. It may be definite الصلة or indefinite الصفة.

Example:

This is *the* girl I met last week. *or* This is *a* girl I met last week.

English does not use a specific conjunction to introduce the relative clause; Arabic, however, does, at least for definite nouns. Relative clauses added to indefinite nouns do not require the relative pronoun. This becomes an obstacle for students, who frequently omit the relative pronoun or use it when it is not necessary. Depending on the gender and number of the definite noun, a specific relative pronoun must be added. So, look at the noun one more time and then decide whether you need the pronoun or not!

Relative pronouns:

after sing. masc. noun	الذي
after sing. fem. noun and non-human plurals	التي
after masc. human plurals	الذِينَ
after fem. human plurals	اللواتي
after masc. dual	الذانِ / الذَيْنِ
after fem. dual	التانِ / التَيْنِ
in colloquial Arabic	اللي

Note that students almost always forget to add the connecting pronoun to the relative pronoun. This is needed when the noun of the main clause is not the subject of the relative clause. In this case, the relative clause needs a pronoun that connects the two pieces. Again, this is something we do not do in English, but it is extremely important in Arabic and can occur regardless of whether we use the relative pronoun or not.

English: This is the girl I met last week.
Girl = noun to modify; I = subject of the relative clause.

In the Arabic sentence we have to add the reference pronoun. In a literal translation, it would read "This is the girl I met *her* last week".

Arabic: هذه هي البنت التي قابلتها الاسبوع الماضي

Examples:

This is the book I bought from Amazon.
هذا هو الكتاب الذي اشتريتُهُ من أمازون.

I read an article on al-Jazeera that talked about the events in Syria.
قرأتُ مقالة في الجزيرة تكلمتْ عن الأحداث في سوريا.

Word order and sentence structure تركيب الجمل 107

I have a friend who studies Arabic.
لي زميل يدرس عربي.

The film we watched last night was very good.
الفلم الذي شاهدناه ليلة أمس كان جيداً جداً.

We live in an apartment that consists of two floors and five rooms.
نسكن في شقة تتكون من طابقين وخمس غرف.

The girl I met in the club was from Yemen.
البنت التي تعرفتُ عليها في النادي كانت من اليمن.

These are the guys who helped me with the project.
هؤلاء الشباب الذين ساعدوني بالمشروع.

What is the name of the company that you are working for?
ما اسم الشركة التي تعمل بها؟

Tomorrow I will go to a store that sells all kinds of electronic gadgets.
غدا أذهب إلى محل يبيع جميع أنواع الأجهزة الإلكترونية.

My mother is a person who influenced me a lot.
والدتي هي الشخص الذي أثر فيّ كثيرا.

Exercise

EXERCISE 7. Decide whether we need a relative pronoun or not.

١) زرتُ الصديق _____ تعرفتُ عليه منذ شهر.
٢) هم أصحاب _____ جاؤوا من السعودية.
٣) حكيتُ مع جاري _____ يسكن بجانبي.
٤) سمعتُ أغنية _____ لم أسمعْها منذ طفولتي.
٥) هذه هي الأستاذة _____ فشلتُ الامتحان معها.
٦) لي أخت _____ اسمها يسرى.
٧) ذكرتُ هذا من كتاب _____ قرأتُهُ الأسبوع الماضي.
٨) كانت السيارة _____ اشتريتُها أمس غالية جدا.
٩) ما هو احسن فلم _____ شاهدتَهُ؟
١٠) أعرف مكاناً _____ أريد أن أذهب إليه.
١١) رحّب الرئيس بالضيوف _____ حضروا الاجتماع.
١٢) تعرفتُ على لاعبين _____ جاؤوا من كل أنحاء العالم.

7 Exception clauses جملة الاستثناء

In order to express an exception, several conjunctions are used. The most common is إلا and translates "except". Other words of exception include ما عدا and غير. They may be followed by a single noun, a phrase or a complete sentence. Note that the word which refers to the exception often isn't even mentioned. Then "only" is translated in the sentence.

Examples:

All the guests attended the party except for his uncle.
حضر الحفلة جميع الضيوف إلا عمه.

I am not afraid (of anything) except my father.
or I am only afraid of my father.
لا أخاف إلا والدي.

We like Arabic food except for raw *kibbe*.
نحب الأكل العربي إلا كبة نية.

All the children swam in the pool except for Fatima.
سبح جميع الأطفال في المسبح إلا فاطمة.

Nothing is in the house except for an old chair.
لا شيء في البيت إلا كرسي قديم.

He greeted the entire family except for his cousin Saud.
سلّم على الأهل كلهم إلا ابن عمه سعود.

I only drink water.   لا أشرب غير الماء.

I can visit you on any day except Sunday.
ممكن أزورك ما عدا يوم الأحد.

We will not return from this trip before a month.
or We will return from this trip only after a month.
لن نعود من الرحلة إلا بعد شهر.

There is no other deity except Allah.   لا إله إلا الله

Tip

إلا is also used to tell the time (see Chapter 8, section 3).

Examples:

It is 2:45.   الساعة الثالثة إلا الربع.
It is 10:55.   في الساعة الحادية عشرة إلا خمس دقائق.

Word order and sentence structure تركيب الجمل 109

Exercise

EXERCISE 8. Translate the sentences.

انجليزي	عربي
	دعونا كل الأقارب إلا زوجة عمي حسين.
I only have one question.	
	لم يسجّل في المباريات إلا هدفين.
Nobody said anything except for the president.	
	لا أحبّ الأكل العربي إلا الكنافة.
It is 5:45 p.m.	
	لم يعد الى الوطن إلا بعد سنتين.
Only they will know.	
	أشهد أن لا امرأة إلا أنت (نزار قباني).
I am not afraid of any animals except for snakes.	

8 Circumstantial clauses جملة الحال

The (in)famous حال clause causes significant problems for non-native speakers because it uses an unfamiliar sentence structure. While it is relatively easy to translate the Haal clause into English (we use the words "while" or "when" to connect the clauses), the other way around is much harder, simply because there are a number of options for translating the sentence into Arabic. Usually non-native speakers choose an option that is closer to their own syntax.

110 Speed Up Your Arabic

> **Tip**
> Refer to the circumstantial clause as the *multi-tasking clause*: doing one thing while doing something else or being something/somewhere when being something/somewhere else.

Examples:

Circumstantial clause	الترجمة ٢ (جملة الحال)	الترجمة ١
He looked at me smiling.	نظر إليّ وهو باسم.	نظر إليّ يتسم.
He eats breakfast while reading the newspaper.	يفطر ويقرأ الجريدة.	يفطر عندما يقرأ الجريدة.
The teacher came with a book in his hand.	جاء الأستاذ وفي يده كتاب.	جاء الأستاذ وكان كتاب في يده.

Exercise

EXERCISE 9. Translate the following circumstantial clauses from Arabic to English and vice versa.

جملة الحال بالإنجليزي	جملة الحال بالعربي
She left him crying.	
	جاء إلى القاهرة صغيراً.
The girl smiles while reading his email.	
	دخل المكتب متأخرا لموعده.
The old man sat in the café drinking his coffee.	
	لا تشرب الماء بارداً!
They listened to the speech without saying a word.	
	سافر إلى الصين نائماً طول الرحلة.
He wrote this poem thinking about his homeland.	
	تركتُ اليمن وأنا طفلة.

9 Questions السؤال

To ask a question in Arabic is not difficult: simply place the question word in front of the sentence. The word order within the sentence is not affected. Two types of question are known, the yes-or-no question and the informative question. The former uses the interrogative particle هل (which students love to omit) and the latter a number of common question words, such as ماذا , أين , ما , كم, sometimes in combination with prepositions, like من , مع , أين , إلى , لماذا , بكم.

Exercise

EXERCISE 10. Ask the right question!

_____ كيلو بندورة بعشرين قرش.
_____ أسكن مع أخي واثنين من أصحابي.
_____ نعم، استمتعتُ به كثيراً.
_____ نسافر إلى تونس هذا الصيف.
_____ أطول بناية في دبي.
_____ طولها كيلو ونصف تقريباً.
_____ اشتريتُه من السوق.
_____ عشتُ في مدينة دمشق.
_____ الآن الساعة الواحدة تماماً.
_____ عمري ثلاثون سنة.
_____ في الغرفة أربعة رجال فقط.
_____ لا، ليس لي أخ.
_____ لم أسمعْ الخبر.
_____ لأنَّهُ كان مريضاً.
_____ درسنا القواعد في الصف أمس.
_____ عيد ميلادي في الأول من سبتمبر.
_____ ولدتُ في سنة ١٩٨٣.
_____ البنت التي كانت معي في النادي هي بنت عمي.
_____ لا، ما عندي وقت.
_____ لا، أظن أنَّهُ خطأ.
_____ لا أريد أي شيء.

8 Numbers
الأرقام والأعداد

1 Cardinal numbers الأعداد الأصلية   113
2 Ordinal numbers الأعْداد الترتيبية   118
3 Using numbers in context   120

113 الأرقام والأعداد *Numbers*

In order to use Arabic numbers properly, it is necessary to know two different sets of numbers: the cardinal and ordinal numbers. Both sets are based on distinct patterns and follow specific rules of agreement and word order. One of the most common errors in Arabic is to mix the use of cardinal and ordinal numbers, for example, students often confuse "one hour" with "the first hour". In this chapter you will learn how to differentiate between cardinal and ordinal numbers and when to use each set of numbers. Other areas of concern are agreement rules between number and noun as well as the correct expression of time and date.

Note that aside from the singular and plural, Arabic uses another type of number, the two-form or dual. Specific rules for how to use the dual with nouns, adjectives, pronouns and verbs apply. Don't forget to use the dual. You will learn how to articulate it with all the words in a sentence.

For the use of the dual, see Chapter 4, section 1.1, Chapter 5, section 5 and Chapter 6, section 5.

1 Cardinal numbers الأعداد الأصلية

Arabic numbers are written as follows:

0	1	2	3	4	5	6	7	8	9	10
٠	١	٢	٣	٤	٥	٦	٧	٨	٩	١٠
صِفْر	واحِد	اِثْنان	ثَلاثَة	أَرْبَعَة	خَمْسَة	سِتَّة	سَبْعَة	ثَمانِيَة	تِسْعَة	عَشَرَة

Unlike Arabic letters, numbers are not written from right to left, but rather from left to right, as in English:

2,012	٢٠١٢	ألفان واثنا عشر
12,956	١٢٩٥٦	إثنا عشر ألفاً وتسعُمائة وستة وخمسون
4.09	٤٫٠٩	أربعة فاصلة صفر تسعة
569–0894	٥٦٩٠٨٩٤	خمسة ستة تسعة صفر ثمانية تسعة أربعة

Note that the comma in large numbers is omitted. Also, a comma is used instead of a decimal point in Arabic.

Numbers one and two are adjectives and agree with the noun in gender, number, state, and case. However, number one is normally not used for counting; instead the noun is used alone, sometimes with the case marker for the indefinite مرفوع (see Chapter 5, section 1):

one car   سيارةٌ   one house   بيتٌ

114 *Speed Up Your Arabic*

The number two is not used for counting; instead the two-form of something is expressed by the dual (المُثَنَّى) and the case endings (انِ / يَْنِ).

بيت ← بيتانِ / بيتَيْنِ   سيارة ← سيارتانِ / سيارتَيْنِ

Numbers three to ten are diptote nouns (see Chapter 4, section 1). Usually, their endings are omitted. All numbers from one to ten have a masculine and a feminine form. For abstract counting, the masculine forms of one and two are used and the feminine forms of three to ten.

From three to ten, the number precedes the indefinite *plural* noun. However, the gender of the number must be opposite to the gender of the noun, i.e. a masculine noun goes with a feminine number and vice versa. Number and noun are part of the إِضافة where the noun is indefinite and مجرور.

Feminine noun with masculine number		Masculine noun with feminine number
ثلاثُ طالباتٍ	٣	ثلاثةُ طلابٍ
أربعُ طالباتٍ	٤	أربعةُ طلابٍ
خمسُ طالباتٍ	٥	خمسةُ طلابٍ
ستُّ طالباتٍ	٦	ستةُ طلابٍ
سبعُ طالباتٍ	٧	سبعةُ طلابٍ
ثماني طالباتٍ	٨	ثمانيةُ طلابٍ
تسعُ طالباتٍ	٩	تسعةُ طلابٍ
عَشْرُ طالباتٍ	١٠	عشرةُ طلابٍ

Except for 12, the numbers 11 to 19 are not grammatically inflected. The number still precedes the noun, but the noun is a *singular* noun case-marked as indefinite منصوب. There is gender agreement between the noun and the "ten", but not between the noun and the single digit.

Number and feminine noun		Number and masculine noun
إحدى عشرةَ طالبةً	١١	أحدَ عشرَ طالباً
إِثنتا عشرةَ طالبةً	١٢	إثنا عشرَ طالباً
ثلاثَ عشرةَ طالبةً	١٣	ثلاثةَ عشرَ طالباً
أربعَ عشرةَ طالبةً	١٤	أربعة عشرَ طالباً
خمسَ عشرةَ طالبةً	١٥	خمسة عشرَ طالباً
ستَّ عشرةَ طالبةً	١٦	ستةَ عشرَ طالباً

115 الأرقام والأعداد *Numbers*

		Number and masculine noun		Number and feminine noun
	١٧	سبعة عشرَ طالباً		سبعَ عشرةَ طالبةً
	١٨	ثمانية عشرَ طالباً		ثماني عشرةَ طالبةً
	١٩	تسعة عشرَ طالباً		تسعَ عشرةَ طالبةً

Note the different spelling of number 12, which has a dual ending and thus drops the final letter ن. It also follows the dual inflection rules:

Twelve students are in class.
في الجامعة اِثنا عشرَ طالباً.

I study with 12 students in class.
أدرسُ في الجامعةِ مع اِثنَيْ عشرَ طالباً.

Twelve (fem.) students are in class.
في الصفِ اِثنتا عشرة طالبةً.

I study with 12 (fem.) students in class.
أدرسُ في الصفِ مع اِثنَيْ عشرة طالبةً.

From 20 to 99, the number is followed by an indefinite *singular* noun in the منصوب case. The decades are considered sound masculine plurals (ونَ and ينَ). The pattern is one-and-twenty, two-and-twenty, three-and-twenty, etc. The numbers 21, 22, 31, 32, etc. show gender agreement with the noun, while the other numbers use the gender opposite to that of the noun.

		Number and masculine noun		Number and feminine noun
	٢٠	عشرونَ طالباً		عشرونَ طالبةً
	٢١	واحدٌ وعشرونَ طالباً		إحدى وعشرونَ طالبةً
	٢٢	إثنان وعشرونَ طالباً		إثنتان وعشرونَ طالبةً
	٢٣	ثلاثةٌ وعشرونَ طالباً		ثلاثٌ وعشرونَ طالبةُ
	٣٠	ثلاثونَ طالباً		ثلاثونَ طالبةً
	٣١	واحدٌ وثلاثونَ طالباً		إحدى وثلاثونَ طالبةً
	٣٢	إثنان وثلاثونَ طالباً		إثنتان وثلاثونَ طالبةً
	٣٣	ثلاثةٌ وثلاثونَ طالباً		ثلاثٌ وثلاثونَ طالبةً
	٤٠	أربعونَ طالباً		أربعونَ طالبةً
	٩٠	تسعونَ طالباً		تسعونَ طالبةً

116 Speed Up Your Arabic

The hundreds, thousands, millions, etc. form an إضافة with a *singular*, indefinite noun. The words "three hundred, four hundred, five hundred", etc. are also إضافة. The rule of opposite agreement applies, i.e. a feminine noun goes with a masculine number. However, note that the word "hundred" is singular although it is preceded by 3 to 9, which usually require the plural noun. Also, the single digit and the hundred are written together as one word.

100 students	مائةُ طالبٍ
200	مائتانِ
200 students	مائتا طالبٍ
300	ثلاثُمائةٍ
900 students	تسعُمائةِ طالبٍ
1,000 students	ألفُ طالبٍ
2,000	ألفانِ
2,000 students	ألفا طالبٍ
3,000	ثلاثةُ آلافٍ
3,000 students	ثلاثةُ آلافِ طالبٍ
1,000,000 students	مليونُ طالبٍ

The word order of larger compound numbers is thousands – hundreds – ones – tens. They are connected by و. Note that whenever the numbers 3 to 10 occur, the gender agreement is reversed.

103	مائةٌ وثلاثُ طالباتٍ
112	مائةٌ واثنا عشر طالباً
200	مائتا طالبٍ
210	مائتانِ وعشرةُ طلابٍ
579	خمسُمائةٍ وتسعةٌ وسبعونَ طالباً
4,817	أربعةُ آلافٍ وثمانِمائةٍ وسبعَ عشرةَ طالبةً
22,222	إثنانِ وعشرونَ ألفاً ومائتانِ اثنتانِ وعشرون طالبةً
1,549,306	مليونٌ وخمسُمائةٍ وتسعةٌ وأربعونَ ألفاً وثلاثُمائةٍ وستةُ طلابٍ

Note also the unique way of counting for 101, 102, 1,001, 1,002, etc.:

101 students	مائةُ طالبٍ وطالبٌ	1,001 nights	ألفُ ليلةٍ وليلةٌ
102 students	مائةُ طالبٍ وطالبانِ	1,002 nights	ألفُ ليلةٍ وليلتانِ

The word order in the definite phrase with numbers is different:

5 students	خمسةُ طلابٍ
the 5 students	الطلابُ الخمسةُ
13 students	ثلاثَ عشرةَ طالبةً
the 13 students	الطالباتُ الثلاثَ عشرةَ

Exercises

EXERCISE 1. Do the math!

٤ زائد ٨ يساوي كم؟ _____

٢٠ ناقص ١٣ يساوي كم؟ _____

٥٥ على ١١ يساوي كم؟ _____

٧ في ٩ يساوي كم؟ _____

في ٣ ساعات كم دقيقة؟ _____

اشتريت الكتاب بستة ريالات ونصف ودفعت بعشرة ريالات. كم الباقي؟ _____

٣٣ + ٢٩ - ٥ = ؟ _____

واحد دولار يساوي ٣٫٧٥ ريال سعودي. كم يساوي واحد ريال بالدولار؟ _____

زرت قطر والبحرين وعمان. كم دولة عربية تبقى قبل أن أزور كلها؟ _____

كم ساعة تدرس اللغة العربية كل يوم؟ _____

EXERCISE 2. Combine the number and noun.

٨ سيارة	____	١١ شهر	____	٥ صلاة	____
٣ بيت	____	١٠ نقطة	____	٢٢ سنة	____
١٢ مدينة	____	١١٢ غرفة	____	٢٠٦٩ نسخة	____
٢ قلم	____	٤٥ طالبة	____	١٢٥٠٩ طفل	____
٢١ شخص	____	٢٠٢ صفحة	____	٣٠ أسبوع	____
٩٩٩ ريال	____	١ حبة	____	١٠٠١ ليلة	____

118   Speed Up Your Arabic

2 Ordinal numbers الأعْداد الترتيبية

As the name suggests, ordinal numbers, such as first, second, third, etc. are used to put things in order. Grammatically they are adjectives derived from the cardinal numbers by using the pattern (الفاعِل / الفاعِلة).

Mnemonic device
English ordinal numbers follow a pattern by adding a suffix (-st, -nd, -rd, or -th). Arabic ordinal numbers follow a pattern too, see above!

Ordinal numbers also follow the noun and agree in gender, number, state, and case. There is no opposite agreement like we have seen with cardinal numbers. Ordinal numbers mostly occur with a definite noun.

Ordinal number with feminine noun		Ordinal number with masculine noun	
the first year	السنةُ الأولى	the first day	اليومُ الأوَّلُ
the second year	السنةُ الثانيةُ	the second day	اليومُ الثاني
the third year	السنةُ الثالثةُ	the third day	اليومُ الثالِثُ
the 11th year	السنةُ الحاديةَ عشْرةَ	the 11th day	اليومُ الحاديَ عَشَرَ
the 12th year	السنةُ الثانيةَ عشْرةَ	the 12th day	اليومُ الثانيَ عشَرَ
the 13th year	السنةُ الثالثةَ عشْرةَ	the 13th day	اليومُ الثالثَ عشَرَ

Note that "first" is not derived from "one". Also note the special form of eleventh. Ordinal numbers between 11 and 19 are not grammatically inflected. The twentieth, thirtieth, fortieth, hundredth, thousandth, etc. use the definite cardinal number equivalent.

Ordinal number with feminine noun		Ordinal number with masculine noun	
the 20th year	السنةُ العشرونَ	the 20th day	اليومُ العشرونَ
the 100th year	السنةُ المائةُ	the 100th day	اليومُ المائةُ
the 1000th year	السنةُ الألفُ	the 1000th day	اليومُ الألفُ

Ordinal compound numbers combine the ordinal number of the ones with the cardinal number of the tens.

119 الأرقام والأعداد *Numbers*

Ordinal number with feminine noun		Ordinal number with masculine noun	
the 21st year	السنةُ الحاديةُ والعشرونَ	the 21st day	اليومُ الحادي والعشرونَ
the 22nd year	السنةُ الثانيةُ والعشرونَ	the 22nd day	اليومُ الثاني والعشرونَ
the 23rd year	السنةُ الثالثةُ والعشرونَ	the 23rd day	اليومُ الثالثُ والعشرونَ

Ordinal numbers above 100 occur very rarely. They are usually expressed in a prepositional phrase.

the 101st year	السنةُ الاولى بعد المائة
the 105th day	اليومُ الخامسُ بعد المائة

Exercises

EXERCISE 3. Translate the phrases with ordinal numbers.

انجليزي	عربي	انجليزي	عربي
the 1st place	_____	_____	السنة الرابعة
the 5th street	_____	_____	في القرن الحادي والعشرين
the 26th floor	_____	_____	الهدف السابع
the 7th day of the week	_____	_____	المدخل الثاني
for the 100th time	_____	_____	الدرجة الأولى

EXERCISE 4. Turn the cardinal number into an ordinal number and vice versa:

_____	الطابق العشرون	_____	ثلاثة أيام
_____	اليوم الثالث	_____	أسبوعان
_____	السنة الثامنة	_____	خمسة شهور
_____	القرن التاسع عشر	_____	تسع سنوات
_____	الدقيقة الأولى	_____	اثنتا عشرة ساعة
_____	الدورة العاشرة	_____	مائة مرة
_____	الساعة الواحدة	_____	هدف واحد
_____	المدرسة الخامسة	_____	أربعة عشر قرناً

EXERCISE 5. Identify and correct the errors in the usage of ordinal and cardinal numbers.

١) هذا اليوم التاسعة عشر في شهر شباط.
٢) أمس كان خمس طلاب واثنا عشر طالبات في الصف.
٣) فاز الفريق للمرة الأول.
٤) تغادر الطائرة في الساعة الحادي عشرة وخمسة وعشرون دقائق.
٥) اشترت أمي ست وعشرون أشياء مفيدة.
٦) استمع أكثر من مئتان طالب إلى المحاضرة.
٧) شاركت اثنين وثلاثين دول في مباريات كأس العالم.
٨) نعيش في القرن الواحد والعشرون.

3 Using numbers in context

Both cardinal and ordinal numbers are used to express time and date. The hour and the day use ordinal numbers and the minute and the year use cardinal numbers.

What time is it? At what time?

5:05	الساعةُ الخامسةُ وخمسُ دقائق
at 10:42	في الساعةِ الحاديةَ عشرةَ إلا ثماني عشرةَ دقيقة
1:15	الساعةُ الواحدةُ والربع
8:40 p.m.	في الساعةِ التاسعةِ إلا الثلثَ مساءً
12:30	الساعةُ الثانيةَ عشرةَ والنصف
3:50 p.m.	في الساعةِ الرابعةِ إلا عشرَ دقائق بعدَ الظهر

Note that إلا is used to say "less" (*lit.* "except") minutes of the hour. A quarter الرُبع, a third الثُلث, or half النصف of the hour are used like their English equivalents.

In colloquial Arabic, cardinal numbers are used to tell the time:

| 6:00 p.m. | الساعة ستة في المساء |
| 5:30 a.m. | الساعة خمسة ونصّ في الصبح |

What is the date today? ما هو تاريخ اليوم؟

121 الأرقام والأعداد *Numbers*

Examples:

اليوم الخامس من حزيران سنة ألفين وأربع.

٢٠٠٤/٦/٥

اليوم السبت الخامس من حزيران (يونيو) ٢٠٠٤ الموافق السابع عشر من ربيع الآخر ١٤٢٥هـ.

Remember to use the cardinal number for the year. The letter هـ indicates the year according to the Islamic calendar. The *Hijri* calendar is a lunar calendar that started with the Prophet Muhammad's migration (هِجْرة) from Mecca to Medina in the year 622. The Western/Christian calendar is marked by adding the letter م after the year. م stands for the birth (of Jesus): الميلاد.

Examples:

1433	في سنةِ ألفٍ وأربعمائةٍ وثلاثٍ وثلاثين
1989	في عامٍ ألفٍ وتسعمائةٍ وتسعةٍ وثمانين
2012	في سنةِ ألفين واِثنتي عشرة

Both calendars have 12 months, however with different names. Furthermore, the eastern part of the Arab world (المشرق العربي) uses different names for the calendar than the western part (مصر والمغرب العربي). The invisible dividing line is somewhere around the Suez Canal.

The names of the months of the year – أسماء شهور السنة:

الشهر الميلادي في المغرب	الشهر الميلادي في المشرق	الشهر الهجري	عدد
يناير	كانون الثاني	مُحَرَّم	١
فبراير	شُباط	صَفَر	٢
مارس	آذار	رَبيع الأول	٣
أبريل	نيسان	رَبيع الثاني	٤
مايو	أيّار	جُمادى الأولى	٥
يونيو	حزيران	جُمادى الأخيرة	٦
يوليو	تمّوز	رَجَب	٧
أغسطس	آب	شَعْبان	٨
سبتمبر	أيلول	رَمَضان	٩
أكتوبر	تِشرين الأول	شَوّال	١٠
نوفمبر	تشرين الثاني	ذو القَعْدة	١١
ديسمبر	كانون الأول	ذو الحِجة	١٢

Because native speakers forget the names of the months occasionally, they substitute them with the cardinal number and "month", e.g. "the ninth month" instead of أيلول.

Exercises

EXERCISE 6. Write the correct name of the month.

_____	الشهر الخامس في المشرق
ذو الحجة	_____
_____	الشهر الهجري التاسع
كانون الثاني	_____
_____	الشهر الآخر في المغرب
آب	_____
_____	الشهر الهجري الثاني
مارس	_____
_____	الشهر الرابع في المشرق
ربيع الأول	_____

EXERCISE 7. Complete the phrases for time and date.

_____	في الساعة الثانية عشرة مساءً
11:45 a.m.	_____
_____	في الساعة الرابعة والثلث
6:05 p.m.	_____
_____	في الساعة السادسة إلا عشر دقائق
exactly 12:15	_____
_____	في الساعة الواحدة والنصف
3:50 in the afternoon	_____
_____	في الساعة الثامنة وخمس وعشرين دقيقة
7:12 a.m.	_____

123 *الأرقام والأعداد* Numbers

في اليوم الأول من أذار عام ألفين واثني عشر

My father passed away on Jan. 31, 1972.

وُلدت في العشرين من شباط سنة ألف وتسعمائة وأربع وسبعين.

I was born in 1389 H.

أصدر هذا الكتاب في سنة مائتين وثلاث وأربعين ه.

Sarah graduated from high school in 1994.

في عام ألفين وإثني عشر الميلادي الموافق عام ألف وأربعمائة وثلاثة وثلاثين الهجري

The film opened on March 1, 2003.

توفي الشيخ زايد في الثاني من نوفمبر عام ألفين وأربعة.

World War II ended on May 8, 1945.

كَمْ ؟ + المُفْرَد المُنَكَّر المَنْصوب

How many?

How many students are in the class?	كم طالباً في الصف؟
How many books did you buy?	كم كتاباً اِشتريتَ؟
How old are you?	كم عُمرُكَ؟
What is his price?	كم سِعرُهُ؟
What time is it?	كم الساعة؟
How long?	كم من الوقت؟

 Note that an *indefinite singular noun* usually follows the question "How many?"

How much?   بِكَمْ؟

    How much is this book?   بكم هذا الكتاب؟

    How much is a kilo of meat?   بكم كيلو من اللحم؟

    How much did you buy that for?   بكم اِشتريتَ ذلك؟

    This book is only 3 dinar.   هذا الكتاب بثلاثةِ دنانير فقط.

    The kilo is 3.5 dollars.   الكيلو بثلاثةِ دولاراتٍ ونصف.

    I bought it for 55 lira.   اِشتريتُهُ بخمسٍ وخمسين ليرةٍ.

How often?   كَمْ مَرَّةً؟

    once, one time   مَرّة

    twice   مَرَّتانِ

    three times   ثلاثُ مَرّاتٍ

    twenty times   عشرونَ مرةً

Exercises

EXERCISE 8. Translate the phrases and expressions into Arabic.

the four rightly guided caliphs   _____

the five pillars of Islam   _____

two million pilgrims   _____

He lives in room 402.   _____

I have three brothers and two sisters.   _____

I was born on December 22, 1981.   _____

The shop opens at 9:30 a.m. and closes at 10:45 p.m.   _____

The party starts at 4:15 p.m.   _____

A barrel of oil costs $102.50.   _____

A gallon of gasoline costs $3.99.   _____

This week I went to the gym three times.   _____

My dad told me to come home at exactly 8:00 p.m.   _____

Today is February 9, 2012.   _____

125 الأرقام والأعداد *Numbers*

EXERCISE 9. Translate into English.

ليّ أربعة أولاد.

أنا طالب في السنة الثالثة.

كنت اشتغل في هذه الشركة لمدة سنتين.

غادرت الطائرة في الساعة الخامسة صباحاً.

ولدت في عام ألف وتسعمائة وواحد وتسعين.

ثمانية قتلى وعشرات من الجرحى في انفجار انتحاري ببغداد.

فاز الأهلي على الشباب بثلاثة أهداف مقابل هدفين.

نلتقي في الساعة السادسة وخمس وعشرين دقيقة.

درجة الحرارة في القاهرة اليوم سبع وثلاثون درجة والرطوبة خمسة وثمانون بالمائة.

الكتاب بتسعة عشر دولارا وتسعة وتسعين سنتا فقط!

EXERCISE 10. Add the correct numbers to complete the sentences.

ولدتُ في _____ (١٥) من شهر تشرين الـ _____(٢) عام _____(١٩٨٣) في مدينة بيروت. لي _____(٤) إخوة وأخت. دخلتُ المدرسة الابتدائية في _____(٦) من عمري. درستُ فيها لمدة _____(٤) سنوات. في عام _____(١٩٩٠) تخرجتُ من المدرسة الثانوية. في الجامعة درستُ الهندسة لمدة _____(٤) سنوات واللغة الفرنسية لمدة _____(٢) سنتين. في عام _____(١٩٩٤) سافرتُ إلى كندا وبقيتُ فيها _____(١٠) أسابيع. في الأسبوع _____(١) وجدتُ وظيفة مناسبة في شركة تجارية وقررتُ البقاء فيها _____(٦) أشهر على الأقل ولكن بالصراحة بقيتُ هناك فترة قصيرة فقط يعني أقل من _____(٤) أسابيع. ثم رجعتُ إلى الوطن بسبب زواجي. زوجتي عمرها _____(٢٢) سنة وهي تعمل مترجمة في نفس الشركة التجارية. هي تتكلم _____(٥) لغات. اللغة _____(٦) التي تدرسها الآن هي اللغة الصينية. نعمل في نفس البناية ومكتبها في الطابق _____(٢٣) ومكتبي في الطابق _____(١١). كل يوم نلتقي _____(٣) مرات وبعد نهاية الدوام نعود إلى البيت في الساعة _____(٥) _____(٤٥) دقيقة.

9 Phrases, idioms and other key words
الأقوال والأمثال، العبارات والمصطلحات

1 Loan words	127
2 New words	128
3 Proverbs and sayings	129
4 Expressions with "God"	130
5 Geographical names and phrases with colors	130
6 Adverbs الظَرف	131
7 Introductory phrases	132
7.1 Other phrases with the elative	133
8 أنْ and أنَّ	134
9 Quantifiers and other similar expressions: كُل , جَميع , عِدّة , بَعْض , مُعْظَم , أحَد , نَفْس	135
10 Similarity مِثل , كَ , كَما , كَأنَّ	138
11 Other useful phrases and key words	139
11.1 عَدَم and غَير	139
11.2 حَتى	140

THE SKY DOESN'T RAIN GOLD = MONEY DOESN'T GROW ON TREES

Phrases, idioms and other key words الأقوال والأمثال، العبارات والمصطلحات

مَن يُخطئ هو إنسان ومَن يَعفو فهو مَلك

Idiomatic expressions, proverbs, standard phrases and other key words are essential for proper language comprehension. They are often not translated literally. So it can be challenging for the learner to know how and when to use them. They also include a cultural component which requires additional study of customs and immersion in the target culture. And they may contain more than one meaning, which makes it mandatory to know how to use them correctly and in the right context. Arabic is *very* rich in these expressions. And since Arabic is a very standardized language, idioms constitute an important part of daily and formal speech.

1 Loan words

Generally, Arabic has influenced other languages more than it has been influenced by them. The language has, however, occasionally borrowed words from languages such as Greek, Persian and Turkish, but has retained most of its vocabulary from Classical Arabic. In recent times, English loan words have found their way into daily speech. However, only rarely can we find corresponding idioms, expressions that exist in both Arabic and English or idioms that are literal loan translations.

Exercise

EXERCISE 1. Try to translate the following examples.

_____	الحرب الباردة
_____	الجدران لها آذان
_____	دموع التماسيح
_____	الحب أعمى
_____	أسلحة الدمار الشامل
_____	عيد الشكر

Direct translation or simple transliteration of idioms, however, is becoming more and more acceptable, especially in media Arabic, political speeches and technical expressions.

Exercise

EXERCISE 2. I am sure you can read and translate these examples.

	ساندويتش		كمبيوتر
	التنس		ديموقراطية
	تكنولوجية		سينما
	تليفون		بترول

2 New words

Although Arabic is an old language it is also a lively language that constantly adjusts to outside input or inside pressure. This flexibility allows for the creation of new words, a task that is very much needed in our time of innovation, exchange and globalization. There are some linguists and traditionalists who like to preserve the historic character of Arabic and support indigenous solutions when introducing new words instead of simply borrowing from English. Before the IT revolution, the Arabic Language Academies were active in the formation of Arabic answers to new words like vacuum cleaner (المكنسة الكهربائية – electric broom) or satellite (القمر الصناعي – industrial moon). Today it is much more difficult first to come up with an original phrase and second to convince the masses to use it. Thus, most Arabs will use (إيميل) instead of (الحاسوب) and (كمبيوتر) instead of (الرسالة الالكترونية). For the non-native speaker this often makes it easier because English loan words have become more common, especially among the younger generation. But don't be fooled: this only works for a few words and they are still used according to Arabic syntax!

Examples:

The word *emails* indicates a non-human plural. Thus it should be used like a feminine singular noun.
I got many emails.
وصلتني ايميلات كثيرة.

A broken plural pattern is used for the plural of doctor.
doctor pl. doctors
دكتور ج دكاترة

Phrases, idioms and other key words الأقوال والأمثال، العبارات والمصطلحات 129

3 Proverbs and sayings

Arabic is rich with sayings, poems and proverbs, and every Arab is able to recite them instantly. Students of Arabic can make a strong impression when they incorporate some popular proverbs into their vocabulary and use them appropriately. Occasionally, these sayings are of universal nature and can be found in English (and other languages) too. At other times, when translated literally they do not make much sense at the beginning and need cross-cultural explanations. Compilations of proverbs for both MSA and the dialects are available, so I will only list a few:

Choose your neighbor before a house and your companion before a road.
الجار قبل الدار والرفيق قبل الطريق.

He who doesn't know the falcon will roast him.
اللي ما يعرف الصقر يشويه.

He who digs a hole will fall in it.
من حفر حفرة وقع فيها.

Some days are like honey, others are like onions.
يوم عسل ويوم بصل.

What happened in the past is gone.
اللي فات مات.

Exercise

EXERCISE 3. Translate the following proverbs with the help of a dictionary and find the English equivalents.

من خاف العصفور ما زرع _____

عصفور باليد أحسن من اثنين في الشجرة _____

يضرب عصفورين بحجر واحد _____

القرش الأبيض ينفع في اليوم الأسود _____

من جدَّ وَجَد _____

الولد ولد لو صار قاضي البلد _____

أنفك منك ولو كان أجْدع _____

إن كنتَ كذوباً فَكُن ذكوراً _____

130 *Speed Up Your Arabic*

4 Expressions with "God"

Arabic, as a religious language, is very rich in idiomatic expressions that evoke the name of God.

OMG!	يا الله
May God be with you.	ألله مَعَك
In God's protection (farewell)	في أمانِ الله
God willing.	إن شاء الله
Praise be to God.	الحمدُ لله
God has willed it.	ما شاء الله
May God forgive me.	استغفِر الله
Glory be to God.	سُبحان الله
May God greet him.	حيّاك الله
May God have mercy on him.	الله يَرحَمُه
May God bless you.	ألله يُبارِك فيك.
In the Name of God the Most Gracious, the Most Merciful	بسم الله الرحمن الرحيم

5 Geographical names and phrases with colors

Casablanca	الدار البيضاء
The Mediterranean Sea (*lit.* "the Middle White Sea")	البحر الأبيض المتوسّط
the black market	السوق السوداء
The Red Indians	الهنود الحمر
The Middle East	الشرق الأوسط
Great Britain	بريطانيا العظمى
the red line	الخط الأحمر
He is good hearted (*lit.* "his heart is white")	قلبه أبيض
He is still interested in women (*lit.* "his soul is green")	نفسه خضراء
bad news (*lit.* "black news")	خبر أسود

Phrases, idioms and other key words الأقوال والأمثال، العبارات والمصطلحات 131

Exercise

EXERCISE 4. Translate the names of the places.

مراكش الحمراء _____

تونس الخضراء _____

الجزائر البيضاء _____

حلب الشهباء _____

البحر الأسود _____

خبر أبيض _____

مدينة الزرقاء _____

الميدالية الذهبية _____

منتخب قطر الوطني – العنابي _____

ساحل العاج _____

6 Adverbs الظَرف

Adverbs modify verbs in time, manner or place. Thus they occur most often in verbal sentences and are located at the end of the sentence. They are derived from the three-letter root and marked by tanwiin of fatHa or appear as a preposition–noun phrase.

Examples:

daily	يومياً	in the morning	صباحاً
northward	شمالاً	never	أبداً
quickly	بِسُرعة	very	جداً
naturally	بشكل طبيعي	usually	عادةً

Note that a common mistake is to mix the two adverbs جداً and كثيراً. Please remember that the first is used to modify adjectives and the second to modify verbs.

Examples:

يأكل أخي كثيراً   هو جوعان جداً

Exercises

EXERCISE 5. Mix and match the following sentences and adverbs: insert an appropriate adverb in each sentence.

مطلقاً (absolutely)	أخي الصغير جوعان
ليلاً ونهاراً (day and night)	يرفضون الاتفاق
سنوياً (annually)	أعرفه
بطيئاً (slowly)	درسنا للتوجيهات
عادةً (usually)	يجتمع الخبراء
جيداً (well)	أحبها
دائماً (always)	يعمل الموظف
كثيراً (a lot)	أصحو في الساعة ٦

EXERCISE 6. What is wrong with these sentences? Correct the word order and use of adverbs.

صواب	خطأ
_____	يقرأ في صباحا الجريدة.
_____	في صيف نسافر دائما الى البحر.
_____	لا يحبون البقلاوة جداً.
_____	كثير أختي القصص القصيرة يقرأ.
_____	في المساءً ينام بسريعاً.
_____	أعرف كلمات عربيات كثيرات.
_____	قريب من بيتها أختي تعمل.
_____	في صباحاً أنا كثير جوعان.

7 Introductory phrases

The following expressions are used to introduce an argument or statement. The phrase consists of the preposition مِن, the article with an adjective (or passive participle) and the conjunction أنْ to introduce a منصوب verb.

It is necessary to	من اللازم أنْ
It is easy to	من السهل أنْ

Phrases, idioms and other key words الأقوال والأمثال، العبارات والمصطلحات 133

It is expected to	مِن المتوقّع أنْ
It is natural to	مِن الطبيعي أنْ
It is possible to	مِن الممكن أنْ
It is stupid to	مِن الغباء أنْ
It is known that	مِن المعروف أنْ
It is kind to	مِن اللطيف أنْ

Remember that كانَ is used to express the phrase in the past tense and ليسَ to negate it in the present tense.

Exercise

EXERCISE 7. Complete the following sentences using your own phrases with "مِن الـ . . . أنْ".

It is necessary to _____
It was wrong to _____
It is strange to _____
It is worth mentioning that _____
It was nice to _____
It wasn't hard to _____
It is important to _____
It is impossible to _____

7.1 Other phrases with the elative

See Chapter 4, section 5.4.

The following phrases are common expressions to modify or introduce Arabic sentences.

at least	على الأقلّ
at most	على الأكثر
to the fullest extent	إلى أقصى حد
mostly	في أغلب الأحيان
as mentioned above	أعلاهُ
underneath, below, at the bottom	في الأسفل
above, at the top	في الأعلى

8 أَنْ and أَنَّ

These two particles are tricky to distinguish, especially in unvocalized texts. But they are clearly used and pronounced differently. If you look at the surrounding words carefully, you will note that أَنْ is always followed by another verb and أَنَّ by a noun or pronoun. Knowing this allows you to read the words properly.

أَنْ connects two verbs. The second verb is in the special المنصوب case, which ends in fatHa or drops the final nuun in some cases.

Examples:

They want to join this team.	يريدون أَنْ يلتحقوا بهذا الفريق.
She decided to live on her own.	قررتْ أَنْ تعيشَ وحدها.

أَنَّ connects two sentences and introduces a nominal sentence, the one that has to start with a noun or pronoun.

Examples:

I think that it is correct.

أظن أنّه صحيح.

We heard in the news that the game ended in a tie.

سمعنا في الأخبار أنّ المباراة انتهت بالتعادل.

Here is a list of common verbs that require either أَنْ or أَنَّ:

الفعل + أنْ + الفعل المنصوب	الفعل + أنّ + الجملة الاسمية
أحبّ أنْ	سمع أنّ
أراد أنْ	قرأ أنّ
أستطاع أنْ	علم أنّ
رفض أنْ	ظن أنّ
يمكن أنْ	تذكر أنّ
قرّر أنْ	قال إنّ
تمنّى أنْ	فهم أنّ

The conjunctions لكنّ and لأنّ require the same nominal sentence. As you remember, nominal sentences can start with a noun or pronoun. But if the following sentence is a verbal sentence, you have to add the equivalent pronoun to the conjunction.

Phrases, idioms and other key words الأقوال والأمثال، العبارات والمصطلحات   135

Examples:

I heard that he bought a new car.
سمعتُ أنَهُ اِشترى سيارة جديدة.

She is tired, but she still works a lot.
إنها تعبانة ولكنها ما زالت تعمل كثيرا.

We understood the film because we visited the place last year.
فهمنا الفلم لأننا زرنا المكان السنة الماضية.

Exercise

EXERCISE 8. Add the correct word, either أنْ or أنَّ. Make sure that you add any necessary pronouns.

١) يريد ____ يذهب إلى هناك.

٢) يمكنني ____ أخرج معكم.

٣) ظننتُ ____ الفلم كان طويلاً ومملاً.

٤) تقول ريمة ____ لا تحضر الحفلة.

٥) قرأنا في الجريدة ____ الاقتصاد أحسن من السنة الماضية.

٦) استطاع الجيش ____ يدخل هذه المنطقة.

٧) سمعوا في الأخبار ____ الرئيس استقال.

٨) شعرتْ البنت ____ ليست جميلة مثل صاحباتها.

9 Quantifiers and other similar expressions:
كُل , جَميع , عِدّة , بَعْض , مُعْظَم , أحَد , نَفْس

It seems to be an issue of vocabulary comprehension, but students almost exclusively rely on كُل as the only quantifier, ignoring other options. These Arabic quantifiers are nouns used as the first word in the إضافة. Please note that the following words can differ in number and/or status.

كُل

كُل means "all", but depending on the status and number of the following noun, it can also be translated as "every" or "as well as".

136 *Speed Up Your Arabic*

every day	كل يوم
all day long	كل اليوم
every day	كل الأيام
Saturday as well as Sunday	كل من يومي السبت والاحد
all of them	كلهم

جَميع

جَميع also means "all". However, it is only used with definite plurals or as an adverb.

all possibilities	جميع الامكانيات
All of us attended the conference.	حضرنا المؤتمر جميعاً.

عِدّة

عِدّة means "several". It must be used with an indefinite plural noun.

after several times	بعد عدة مرات
Several questions were asked.	طُرحت عدة أسئلة.

بَعْض

بَعْض means "some". It is followed by either a definite plural noun or a personal suffix.

some days	بعض الأيام
some participants	بعض المشاركين
some of them	بعضهم
They helped each other.	ساعدوا بعضهم البعض.

مُعْظَم

مُعْظَم means "most (of)" and is used with a definite plural noun.

Most (of the) students study several hours every day.

معظم الطلاب يدرسون عدة ساعات كل يوم.

Most of them are diligent.

معظمهم مجتهدين.

Phrases, idioms and other key words الأقوال والأمثال، العبارات والمصطلحات

أَحَد (مِن)

أَحَد (مِن) means "one of". It is used with definite plural nouns.

I asked one of those in charge.	سألتُ أحد المسؤولين.
I asked one of them.	سألتُ أحدهم.
I asked one of you.	سألتُ أحد منكم.

نَفْس

The literal meaning of نَفْس ج أَنْفُس , نُفُوس is "soul". However, if you use it with another noun it will create إضافة and its meaning changes to "the same". If it follows a noun, it should carry a corresponding pronoun reference to that noun and its case as well. Now it refers to the concept of *myself – on my own, yourself, himself*.

Examples:

We study at the same university.	ندرس في نفس الجامعة.
We study at the university by ourselves.	ندرس في الجامعة بأنفسنا.
I arrived there on the same day.	وصلتُ إلى هناك في نفس اليوم.
I arrived there on my own.	وصلتُ إلى هناك بنفسي.

Exercise

EXERCISE 9. Translate the following sentences and use the correct quantifier.

I invited several friends to the party.	دعوتُ
Last week I wrote some of my friends.	كتبتُ
My mom bought the same dress.	إشترتْ
We went to the store several times.	ذهبنا
I spent the entire day cleaning my room.	قضيتُ
We arrived at our hotel after several hours.	وصلنا
All of the guests came to the party.	جاء
Some people don't like this book.	لا يحب
During the summer break every day was beautiful.	كانتْ
One of the guys was very kind.	كان
All of them were there.	كان

She completed the project herself.	اِنجزتْ
The president talked to the foreign minister as well as the finance minister.	تكلّم
I read the entire book.	قرأتُ
Did you do that by yourself?	هل فعلتَ
Every day I get up at 6 a.m.	أصحو
Most of my relatives live in Jordan.	يعيش
Yesterday I met one of them.	قابلتُ
Do you have everything?	هل عندك
They ate some of the food.	أكلوا

10 Similarity: مِثل , كَ , كَما , كأنَّ

As with the quantifiers, Arabic words for similarity can be recognized by the word that succeeds them, i.e. the next word in the sentence. Although they might express the same meaning ("like", "as"), they modify different word types (nouns, pronouns or verbs). Too often students mix them up. However, it is merely a question of vocabulary training and syntax observation to distinguish between them.

Examples:

as usual	كالعادة
as if nothing happened	كأن شيئًا لم يكن
as I said earlier	كما قُلتُ سابقاً
like everyone else	مثل أي شخص آخر
I wish I was strong like him.	أتمنى أن أكون قوياً مثله.

Exercise

EXERCISE 10. Translate the following sentences.

أنت بطئ كالسُلَحْفاة.
_____

I am not like you.   _____

سيارة فيراري سريعة كالريح.
_____

Phrases, idioms and other key words الأقوال والأمثال، العبارات والمصطلحات

As you all know this is not right.	
_____	أحمد طبيب مثل والدِهِ.
You behave like a little boy.	
_____	أنا طالب مثلَهُ.
As you wished.	

11 Other useful phrases and key words

11.1 غَيْر and عَدَم

These two words express the negating prefix of "un-", "non-" or "il-" in words like "unholy", "unlikely", "illegal", "illogical", "non-binding", etc. They can also help you to come up with opposites.

> **Tip**
> If you forget an adjective, but you do remember the opposite, you can express the former by using the latter in connection with "un-", "not" or "non-". For example, if you forget how to say "clean" you can say "not dirty":
>
> نظيف – غير نظيف = وسخ
> نظافة – عدم نظافة = وساخة

Here's how it works: غير negates adjectives and عدم negates nouns.

Examples with غير:

unlikely	غير محتمل
untrue	غير صحيح
nonprofit organization	منظمة غير ربحية
spam (undesired mail)	بريد غير مرغوب
illegal	غير شرعي
unhappy people	الناس غير سعداء
non-Saudi	غير سعودي

Examples with عدم:

Please don't smoke.	الرجاء عدم التدخين.
Do not disturb.	عدم الإزعاج.
inability	عدم القدرة
Certificate of Good Conduct	شهادة عدم المحكومية
Non-Aligned Movement	حركة عدم الانحياز
He announced that he is not running for election.	أعلن عدم خوضه الانتخاب.
Please don't throw the garbage away.	رجاءً عدم إلقاء القمامة.

Exercise

EXERCISE 11. Choose the correct negating word, either عدم or غير.

١) شكرا لـ ـــــــ التدخين في الغرفة.
٢) يعمل مع شركة ـــــــ حكومية.
٣) ارتكب الخطأ ـــــــ مقصود.
٤) معهد تعليم اللغة العربية لـ ـــــــ الناطقين بها.
٥) وقع الطرفان معاهدة ـــــــ الاعتداء.
٦) يعاني اللاجئون من ـــــــ وجود الأمن والطعام.
٧) ـــــــ قدرة الطلاب على دفع الأقساط.
٨) صوتها ـــــــ واضح.

11.2 حَتَّى

حتى usually introduces a temporal adverbial clause, but with two quite different translations. If حتى is followed by a past tense verb it means "until" and if it is followed by a present tense verb it means "in order to". The combination حتى ولو translates "even".

Examples:

She worked long hours until she finished her homework.
عملتْ ساعات طويلة حتى أنجزت واجباتها.

He stays at the library in order to finish his homework.
يبقى في المكتبة لينجز واجباته.

Answer key to exercises 143

دليل	✓ ذلك	
العُسر	✓ اليُسر	
هيئة ✓	حيّة	
مكسور ✓ مقصود		

EXERCISE 6.

ش	الليل	ش	الصباح
ش	الرمال	ق	الكرسي
ش	الديموقراطية	ق	المتحف
ش	الضمير	ش	الديوان
ش	الرياض	ش	السماء
ش	التفاح	ق	الورقة
ش	الطائرة	ش	الزبون
ش	الظلم	ق	الاختبار
ق	العيون	ق	الفنون
ش	السياسة	ش	الذهاب

EXERCISE 7.

٢	مُستَقبَل	١	شَجَرة
٣	مُستَقبَلُهُم	٢	أصْحاب
١	قِصَص	٢	مُساعَدة
٣	إقتِصاد	٣	يَزورونهُ
٢	أُحِبّ	١	رَجُل

EXERCISE 8.

a	المدينة الجميلة
a	الحكومة التونسية
at	حكومة دولة قطر
at	سيارة والدي
at	جامعة الدول العربية
a	الجامعة الحكومية
a	الأستاذة فاطمة
a	العلاقة السياسية
a	العلاقة بين الدولتين
at	مدينة الرياض

144 *Answer key to exercises*

EXERCISE 9.
No answer is provided for this exercise.

EXERCISE 10.

safari	السَفر
admiral	أمير البحر
lute	العود
magazine	مَخزن
giraffe	الزرافة
cotton	قُطن
jar	الجَرّ
damask	قُماش دِمَشْقي
alcohol	الكُحول
coffee	قَهوة
adobe	الطوبة
algorithm	الخوارزمي
assassin	حَشيشين
algebra	الجَابر
sugar	سُكر

Chapter 2

EXERCISE 1.

ي	ا	ل	م	ط	ر	و	ل	ا
م	ل	و	م	ه	م	ر	ن	ي
ء	ز	ه	و	س	ا	ف	ء	س
ا	ه	ل	ي	ا	ل	ص	ي	ف
ت	و	ا	غ	ح	ب	ش	ل	ي
ش	ر	ح	ل	ا	ر	ب	ا	ر
ل	و	ب	ا	ب	د	و	ر	خ
ا	ي	ا	ل	ش	م	س	ي	ل
ق	ن	ز	ع	ي	ب	ر	ل	ا

EXERCISE 2.

Part 1

١	حُجاج	٢	أثاث	٣	مُحَمَّد	٤	مُوَظَّف
٥	سياسة	٦	الآن	٧	لَقْلَق	٨	حَديقة
٩	مُمِلّ	١٠	مُمْتِع	١١	مَعْبَد	١٢	أسْلِحة نَوَوية
١٣	عَرَب	١٤	أصْدِقاء	١٥	تَحَضُّر	١٦	جَواب
١٧	جامِعة	١٨	مَوْسِم	١٩	غِياب	٢٠	غُرْفة

Part 2

٢١	سَبَب	٢٢	جُمْهورية	٢٣	صُعوبة	٢٤	مَظْلوم
٢٥	أوْزان	٢٦	مُتَطَلِّبات	٢٧	أساتذة	٢٨	عَدَل
٢٩	مُساعَدة	٣٠	بَرامِج	٣١	مِشْمِش	٣٢	مُطَوَّعون
٣٣	هو	٣٤	سُبُل	٣٥	إجْتِماعات	٣٦	سِكّة حَديدية
٣٧	يَتَذَكَّرونَني	٣٨	العِراق	٣٩	أمامَ	٤٠	ضَفْدَع

EXERCISE 3.

ism (name)	اسم	ukht (sister)	أخت
akhbaar (news)	أخبار	ibn (son)	ابن
ustaadh (professor)	أستاذ	abwaab (doors)	أبواب
bi'r (well)	بئر	qiraa'a (reading)	قراءة
ra'at (she saw)	رأت	ra'iis (president)	رئيس
mas'uul (responsible)	مسؤول	muruu'a (manliness)	مروءة
masaa' (evening)	مساء	mabda' (principle)	مبدأ
lu'lu' (pearl)	لؤلؤ	su' (ill)	سوء
shaaTi' (beach)	شاطيء	zumalaa' (colleagues)	زملاء

EXERCISE 4.

خطأ	صواب
أتمنى لك الصحه والعافيه.	أتمنى لك الصحة والعافية.
في بيته غرف كثيره.	في بيته غرف كثيرة.
مدينته جميله.	مدينته جميلة.
المنبه تحت الوساده.	المنبه تحت الوسادة.
جاء أصحابى الى.	جاء أصحابي إليّ.
فى المقهى كراسي فارغة.	في المقهى كراسي فارغة.

146 Answer key to exercises

EXERCISE 5.

الصديق العزيز: كيف الحال وصحتك أرجو أن تكون بخير وعافية
لقد انقطعت أخباركم عني ولم أعد أسمع عنكم شيئاً ولا أعرف
اخباركم. ففي كل يوم أذهب إلى البريد على أمل أن تأتيني
رسالة منكم ولكن لسوء الحظ لا يوجد شيء أرجو أن لا
يكون هناك عائقاً ومانعاً لذلك وربما إن الدراسة
أو العمل لا يسمح لكم بكتابة رسالة إليّ.

EXERCISE 6.

شجرة	ش + ج + ر + ة	باب	ب + ا + ب
لذيذ	ل + ذ + ي + ذ	حبيب	ح + ب + ي + ب
ورق	و + ر + ق	حقوق	ح + ق + و + ق
ممل	م + م + ل	جديد	ج + د + ي + د
هذه	ه + ذ + ه	تمر	ت + م + ر
دعوة	د + ع + و + ة	كلام	ك + ل + ا + م
شجاع	ش + ج + ا + ع	ألله	أ + ل + ل + ه
أشياء	أ + ش + ي + ا + ء	رئيس	ر + ئ + ي + س
لأنه	ل + أ + ن + ه	ذوي	ذ + و + ي
ظنوا	ظ + ن + و + ا	راديو	ر + ا + د + ي + و

EXERCISE 7.

وصل أحمد إلى مركز المدينة قادماً من بيت **الحماة**. كانت معه **هذه الفتاة** الشابة
التي **سألوا** عنها **دائماً**. ذهبا إلى السوق حيث اشترت **الفتاة** فستاناً جديداً وكتباً.
هناك قابلا صديقة أحمد ورجعوا كلهم إلى بيتهم لأنه جاء وقت **الصلاة**. في البيت
أكلوا طعاماً خفيفاً وتفرجوا الأخبار في قناة الجزيرة **ولكن** بعد ذلك عاد أحمد إلى
شقة عائلته راكباً سيارة الحماة.

EXERCISE 8.

My phone number is 202-4595501.	رقم تليفوني ٤٥٩٥٥٠١–٢٠٢.
In your bank account is 6,550,100.25 dirham.	في حسابك ٦٥٥٠١٠٠,٢٥ درهماً.
The total is 105.05 dinar.	المبلغ الكامل هو ١٠٥,٠٥ ديناراً.
I was born in 1923.	ولدت في ١٩٢٣.
In 1955 Cairo had a population of 5,505,000.	في عام ١٩٥٥ كان عدد سكان القاهرة ٥٥٠٥٠٠٠ نسمة.

Answer key to exercises 147

EXERCISE 9.

خجل	ل + ج + خ	يمحض	ي + م + ح + ض
الألوان	ا + ل + أ + ل + و + ا + ن	لحم	ل + ح + م
لما	ل + م + ا	محل	م + ح + ل
نجيب	ب + ي + ج + ن	نهار	ن + ه + ا + ر

EXERCISE 10.

7aga	حاجة	bitshouf 7alak fiya	بتشوف حالك فيه
3an 2arib	عن قريب	ma3ak	معك
7abibi wenta b3id	حبيبي وأنت بعيد	la7za	لحظة
ya 3eyni 3o2albak	يا عيني (ع)قبلك	3ala 6ul	على طول
ana rayi7 il-jami3a	أنا رايح الجامعة	6aal 3umrak	طال عمرك
9ba7 il-5er	صباح الخير	i6la3	اطلع

Chapter 3

EXERCISE 1.

The baker bakes bread at the bakery.	خَبَزَ الخَبّاز الخُبْز في المِخْبَز.	baking	خ - ب - ز
The player plays the game at the playground.	لعب اللاعب اللعبة في الملعب.	playing	ل - ع - ب
The cook cooks the food in the kitchen.	طبخ الطباخ الطبخ في المطبخ.	cooking	ط - ب - خ
The butcher butchers the meat at the slaughterhouse.	ذبح الذباح الذبيحة في المذبحة.	butchering	ذ - ب - ح
The sender sends the letters in the mail.	أرسل المرسِل الرسالة في المراسلة.	sending	ر - س - ل
The farmer plants the seeds at the farm.	زرع الزارع الزَرع في المزرعة.	planting	ز - ر - ع

148 *Answer key to exercises*

EXERCISE 2.

Description	الوزن	الترجمة	الكلمة
singular masculine adjective	فَعِيل	friendly	لَطِيف
1st person plural, present tense, form II	نُفَعِّل	we smoke	نُدَخِّن
broken plural	فُعَلاء	experts (masc.)	خُبَراء
active participle from verb form V, masculine plural	مُتَفَعِّلون	spectators (masc.)	مُتَفَرِّجون
sound feminine plural	فُعولات	governments	حُكومات
feminine ordinal number	الفاعِلة	the third (fem.)	الثالِثة
3rd person plural, past tense, form I	فَعِلوا	they failed	فَشِلوا

EXERCISE 3.

التَفْكِير

1 It has more than three letters.
2 We need to omit the article.
3 The ر is the third root letter.
4 The ت is a prefix and omitted.
5 The vowel ي is part of the pattern, not the root.

The root is ف – ك – ر (from right to left).

The pattern is تفعيل. It describes the infinitive of Form II.

يُساعِدونَها

1 The word has more than three letters.
2 It has a suffix (ها) to omit.
3 The letters ي and ون mark the verbal pattern.
4 The letter ا marks a verb of Form III.

The root is س – ع – د.

The pattern is يُفاعِلونَها. It describes a third person plural present tense verb with object pronoun.

الاستئجار

1 The word has more than three letters.
2 We must omit the article.
3 The last letter (ر) is the third root letter.
4 The letters ا, س, and ت are part of the pattern.
5 The second ا is not a root letter.

The root is أ – ج – ر.

The pattern is الاستفعال. It describes the infinitive of Form X.

EXERCISE 4.

الكلمة	الوزن	الكلمة	الوزن
يذهب	يَفْعَل	تجميل	تَفْعيل
مبروك	مَفْعُول	سيارة	فَعَالة
صباح	فَعَال	إنجازات	افْعَالات
إجتماع	افْتِعَال	إشتراك	افْتِعَال
سافرنا	فَاعَلْنا	جدد	فُعُل
بحيرة	فُعَيْلة	حقائق	فَعائل

EXERCISE 5.

الكلمة	الجذر ١	الجذر ٢	الجواب الصحيح: ١ أو ٢؟
مدارس	د - ر - س	م - ر - س	١
خطّ	خ - ط - ء	خ - ط - ط	٢
أجهزة	أ - ه - ز	ج - ه - ز	٢
محطّة	م - ح - ط	ح - ط - ط	٢
أبيض	ب - ي - ض	أ - ب - ض	١
صلاة	ص - ل - و	ص - ل - ا	١
كُرة	ك - ر - ر	ك - ر - و	٢
التغيّب	ت - غ - ب	غ - ي - ب	٢
مستقبل	س - ق - ل	ق - ب - ل	٢
يضعون	و - ض - ع	ي - ض - ع	١

EXERCISE 6.

الكلمة	الجذر	الوزن	الترجمة
الجامعة	ج م ع	الفاعِلة	university
التدخين	د خ ن	التَفْعيل	smoking
السبعينات	س ب ع	الفعلينات	the seventies
المساعدة	س ع د	المُفاعَلة	help
كانت	ك و ن	فَعَلَتْ	she did
دقائق	د ق ق	فَعائل	minutes
يشاهدون	ش ه د	يُفاعِلون	they watch
إشتباكات	ش ب ك	افْتِعالات	clashes
وزارة	و ز ر	فِعالة	ministry

150 *Answer key to exercises*

EXERCISE 7.

الترجمة	الكلمة	الوزن	الجذر
bakery	مخبز	مَفْعَل	خ ب ز
long, tall	طويل	فَعِيل	ط و ل
visit	زيارة	فِعَالة	ز و ر
better	أحسن	أَفْعَل	ح س ن
friends	أصحاب	أفْعَال	ص ح ب
problem	مشكلة	مُفْعِلة	الو ز ن
she met	اجتمعت	افْتَعَلَتْ	ج م ع
hearts	قلوب	فُعُول	ق ل ب
observation	مراقبة	مُفَاعَلَة	ر ق ب
smoking	تدخين	تَفْعِيل	د خ ن
colleagues	زملاء	فُعَلاء	ز م ل
popular, beloved	محبوب	مَفْعُول	ح ب ب
photographer	مصوّر	مُفَعِّل	ص و ر
rooms	غرف	فُعَل	غ ر ف

EXERCISE 8.

أفعال		فُعول	
جمع التكسير	مفرد	جمع التكسير	مفرد
أهداف	هدف	ضيوف	ضيف
أبواب	باب	بيوت	بيت
أجداد	جدّ	جيوش	جيش
أخبار	خبر	حدود	حدّ
أشخاص	شخص	حروب	حرب
أصوات	صوت	حروف	حرف
أطراف	طرف	حقوق	حقّ
أطفال	طفل	دروس	درس
أعلام	عَلَم	ردود	ردّ
أعوام	عام	شروط	شرط
أعداد	عدد	شهور	شهر
أفراد	فرد	صفوف	صفّ
أفلام	فلم	علوم	عِلم

Answer key to exercises 151

أفعال			فُعول		
جمع التكسير	مفرد		جمع التكسير	مفرد	
أقسام	قسم		عيون	عين	
أقلام	قلم		فصول	فصل	
أنواع	نوع		فنون	فنّ	
أهداف	هدف		قلوب	قلب	
أوراق	ورقة		كؤوس	كأس	
أوقات	وقت		كنوز	كنز	
أولاد	ولد		ملوك	ملك	

EXERCISE 9.

الترجمة	المكان	الجذر
exit	مخرج	خ – ر – ج
stadium, playground	ملعب	ل – ع – ب
airport	مطار	ط – ي – ر
council, sitting room	مجلس	ج – ل – س
home	منزل	ن – ز – ل
laundromat, launderette	مغسلة	غ – س – ل
bank	مصرف	ص – ر – ف
temple	معبد	ع – ب – د
swimming pool	مسبح	س – ب – ح
entry	مدخل	د – خ – ل

EXERCISE 10.

الترجمة	الكلمة العربية	الترجمة	الكلمة العربية	الترجمة	الكلمة العربية
green (fem.)	خضراء	station	محطة	schools	مدارس
massacre	ملحمة	friends	أصدقاء	I learned	تعلمتُ
opportunities	إمكانيات	the return	العودة	institution	مؤسسة
dirty	وسخ	she woke up	إستيقظتْ	residence	إقامة
they arrive	يصلون	cold	بارد	novel	رواية

152 *Answer key to exercises*

Chapter 4

EXERCISE 1.

رجال عراقيون	كبير	رجل
أقلام جديدة	عراقي	قلم
سيدات لطيفات	مشغول	سيدة
شوارع واسعة	جديد	شارع
أيام مشغولة	لطيف	يوم
ساعات طويلة	واسع	ساعة
لغات أجنبية	طويل	لغة
طلاب كبار	كثير	طالب
جامعات كثيرة	أجنبي	جامعة
طالبات نشيطات	نشيط	طالبة

EXERCISE 2.

الجمع	المفرد
هناك بيوت جديدة.	هناك بيت جديد.
هناك مدارس قديمة.	هناك مدرسة قديمة.
في البيوت غرف كبيرة.	في البيت غرفة كبيرة.
الرسائل طويلة.	الرسالة طويلة.
الصور جميلة.	الصورة جميلة.
في الصفوف زملاء جدد.	في الصف زميل جديد.
هناك معيدون مجتهدون.	هناك معيد مجتهد.
الدروس صحيحة.	الدرس صحيح.
هنا صديقات جميلات.	هنا صديقة جميلة.
الغرف نظيفة.	الغرفة نظيفة.
سياراتك وسخة.	سيارتك وسخة.
في الجامعات أساتذة أجانب.	في الجامعة أستاذ أجنبي.

Answer key to exercises 153

EXERCISE 3.

الاسم	الجنس	الاسم	الجنس	الاسم	الجنس
كلب	M	الوالدة	F	الارض	F
عمارة	F	ولد	M	مُدُن	F
معلمون	M	جميل	M	مترجمات	F
اليوم	M	كُتَيْبة	F	رجال	M
عاصمة	F	الجمهورية	F	أنْتَ	M

EXERCISE 4.

الغرفة + وسخ	الغرفة وسخة.
الرحلة + طويل	الرحلة طويلة.
العدد + كبير	العدد كبير.
الموظفات + مشغول	الموظفات مشغولات.
الأكل + لذيذ	الأكل لذيذ.
البيوت + بعيد	البيوت بعيدة.
الدروس + صعب	الدروس صعبة.
الراتب + مناسب	الراتب مناسب.
درجة الحرارة + عالي	درجة الحرارة عالية.
السياسيون + فاسد	السياسيون فاسدون

EXERCISE 5.

المدينة كبيرة	في هذا المحل كتب كثيرة
يذهب والدي إلى المكتب	عاصمة السعودية هي الرياض
هناك مدرسة جيدة	تلبس نفس الفستان
في البيت خمس غرف	الحكومة السورية
احب أن ادرس اللغات	جماعة الإخوان المسلمين
يحب الشباب الرياضة	نحن في البيت
تقف السيارة أمام البيت	ما فهمت سؤالك
تشرب أختي القهوة في المساء	عندي وقت للذهاب إلى البحر
قضينا اسبوعين في هذا المكان	جامعة الدول العربية
اشاهد التليفزيون في الصباح	يدرس طلاب كثيرون الهندسة

EXERCISE 6.

No answer is provided for this exercise.

154 *Answer key to exercises*

EXERCISE 7.

انجليزي	عربي	انجليزي	عربي
London	لندن	Washington	واشنطن
Europe	اوروبّا	operetta	اوبريت
telephone	تليفون	email	ايميل
bus	اتوبيس	vitamins	فيتامينات
cafeteria	كافيتريا	doctor	دكتور

EXERCISE 8.

الرئيس	مكتب
تليفوني	رقم
البرلمان	عضو
الدولة	عاصمة
كيلو سكر	سعر
المباراة	نهاية
أخي	زوجة
الشركة	مدير
المقالة	ملخص
العالم	كأس

EXERCISE 9.

خطأ أو صواب	إضافة
صواب	كلية الهندسة
صواب	مدينة الكويت
خطأ	بيته الجميل
صواب	مناقشة سبل التعاون
خطأ	المدينة المنورة
صواب	رئيس الوزراء
صواب	غرفة نوم
صواب	دولة قطر
خطأ	أستاذ جامعي
خطأ	الجامعة العربية

Answer key to exercises 155

EXERCISE 10.

اسم فاعل	الفعل الماضي	اسم فاعل	الفعل الماضي
قاتِل	قتل	**مسافِر**	سافر
خائف	خاف	**واقِع**	وقع
مساعِد	ساعد	**متحدِّث**	تحدث
مستثمِر	استثمر	**مستعمِل**	استعمل
مشاهِد	شاهد	**باحِث**	بحث

EXERCISE 11.

اسم مفعول	الفعل الماضي	اسم مفعول	الفعل الماضي
مذكور	ذكر	**مشروع**	شرع
مشترَك	اشترك	**ملحَق**	الحق
موضوع	وضع	**مقصود**	قصد
ملوَّن	لوّن	**مستعمَل**	استعمل

EXERCISE 12.

١) التدخين **ممنوع** (يمنع) في هذه الغرفة.

٢) يقع المطعم **خارج** (يخرج) سور المدينة القديمة.

٣) السيد فرحان هو **الناطق** (ينطق) الرسمي لمجلس الشورى.

٤) أنا **متزوج** (يتزوج) منذ عشر سنين.

٥) بعد التخرج أشتغل **معيداً** (يُعيد) في نفس الكلية.

٦) اللاعب سامي جابر هو **لاعب** (يلعب) **مشهور** (يشهر) في **المنتخب** (ينتخب) السعودي.

٧) صديقتي ريم هي **ساكنة** (يسكن) مع أسرتها في دبي.

٨) أمس شاهدتُ فلماً مع **الممثل** (يمثّل) **المعروف** (يعرف) عادل امام.

٩) أمي **عارفة** (يعرف) أنا **نائم** (ينام).

١٠) الوضع في مصر **مختلف** (يختلف) عن الوضع السوري.

١١) عفواً، الأخ عبد الله **موجود** (وجد)؟

١٢) نعم، ولكن هو **مشغول** (يشغل).

١٣) هذه الطماطم **مستورَدة** (يستورد) من كندا.

١٤) الشركة **المستورِدة** (يستورد) **مقيمة** (يقيم) في دبي.

١٥) المكتبة **مفتوحة** (يفتح) كل يوم حتى الساعة التاسعة.

156 Answer key to exercises

EXERCISE 13.

This is an old house.	هذا بيت قديم.
This house is old.	هذا البيت قديم.
this old house	هذا البيت القديم
This old house is clean.	هذا البيت القديم نظيف.
This is a great idea.	هذه فكرة رائعة.
This idea is great.	هذه الفكرة رائعة.
this great idea	هذه الفكرة الرائعة
This great idea is unique.	هذه الفكرة الرائعة بديعة.
These are expensive books.	هذه كتب غالية.
These books are expensive.	هذه الكتب غالية.
these expensive books	هذه الكتب الغالية
These expensive books are rare.	هذه الكتب الغالية نادرة.
These are young men.	هؤلاء شباب صغار.
These men are young.	هؤلاء الشباب صغار.
these young men	هؤلاء الشباب الصغار
These young men are brave.	هؤلاء الشباب الصغار شجعان.

EXERCISE 14.

١) الحروف **الشمسية والقمرية**. (الشمس، القمر)

٢) الوضع **الاقتصادي** في اليونان صعب جدا. (الاقتصاد)

٣) هذا الجهاز من انتاج **صيني**. (الصين)

٤) العلاقات **التجارية** بين البلدين جيدة. (التجارة)

٥) طرابلس الشرق مدينة **لبنانية** وطرابلس الغرب مدينة **ليبية**. (لبنان، ليبيا)

٦) والدي كان عنده سكتة **قلبية**. (القلب)

٧) دراسات العالم العربي الاسلامي.

٨) عبد الرحمن وأحمد وخالد شباب **سعوديون**. (السعودية)

٩) كلية العلوم **السياسية** (السياسة)

١٠) الجملة **الإسمية** والجملة **الفعلية** (الاسم، الفعل)

Answer key to exercises   157

EXERCISE 15.

أكثر اجتهاداً	مجتهد	أجمل	جميل
أسعد	سعيد	أصعب	صعب
أكثر شعبيةً	شعبي	أبرد	بارد
أكثر عطشاً	عطشان	أصغر	صغير
أحرّ	حارّ	أجدّ	جديد
أوسع	واسع	أحسن	حسن

EXERCISE 16.

the best class	أحسن صف
the prettiest girl	أجمل بنت
the hardest decision	أصعب قرار
the tallest building	أطول عمارة
the last time	آخر مرة
the newest car	أجدّ سيارة
the strangest thing	أغرب شيء
the most distant place	أبعد مكان
the easiest test	أسهل اختبار
the biggest city	أكبر مدينة

EXERCISE 17.

سامر شاب **طويل** جدا، هو **أطول** من وليد ولكن خليل هو **الأطول** بين أصحابه. سامر أيضاً **رفيع** جداً، هو **أرفع** من صالح وهو الشاب **الأطول** في الصف. سامر يجلس على كرسي **كبير**. هذا الكرسي **أكبر** من الكرسي الذي يجلس عليه وليد. سامر **وسيم** ولكن تقول البنات إن وليد **أوسم** منه، وصالح هو **الأوسم**. المشكلة هي سامر **ممتع** ووليد **ممل** وصالح هو **أكثر مللاً** من وليد، في الصراحة صالح هو **الأكثر مللاً** في الصف كله.

Regular adjective	Comparative form	Superlative form
طويل	أطول	الأطول
رفيع	أرفع	الأطول
كبير	أكبر	الأوسم
وسيم	أوسم	الأكثر مللاً
ممتع	أكثر مللاً	
ممل		

158 *Answer key to exercises*

EXERCISE 18.

التفاحة صفراء وحمراء	red and yellow + التفاحة
الموزة صفراء	yellow + الموزة
السماء زرقاء	blue + السماء
الضفدع أخضر	green + الضفدع
الفيل رمادي	gray + الفيل
البرتقال برتقالي	orange + البرتقال
الدب بني	brown + الدب
العلم السعودي أخضر وأبيض	green and white + العلم السعودي
الشعر أشقر	blond + الشعر
العيون زرقاء	blue + العيون

EXERCISE 19.

سيارتكَ سريعة جداً.	(سيارة + أنتَ) سريعة جداً.
والدنا مشغول دائماً.	(والد + نحن) مشغول دائماً.
أقاربها من القدس.	(أقارب + هي) من القدس.
قال له: كيف حالك؟	قال (لـ + هو): كيف (حال + أنت)؟
هل بيتكم قريب من بيتي؟	هل (بيت + أنتم) قريب من (بيت + أنا)؟
ليست غرفتكِ نظيفة!	ليست (غرفة + أنتِ) نظيفة!
نسيت شنطتي في السيارة.	نسيتُ (شنطة + أنا) في السيارة.
أصدقاؤنا من المغرب.	(أصدقاء + نحن) من المغرب.
أين يسكن عمكم؟	أين يسكن (عم + أنتم)؟
صوتها جميل.	(صوت + هي) جميل.

EXERCISE 20.

شيد **الأنباط العرب** في جنوب الأردن حضارة رائعة في القرنين الأول قبل الميلاد، وكانت مدينة البتراء التي <u>نحتوها</u> في الصخر من أروع ما **تركوه**، فقد نحتوا **المعابد والقصور والمقابر**، وشقوا طريقا يوصل إلى هذه المدينة يبلغ **طوله** ٢ كم وهو الطريق المعروف بالسيق.

وفي البتراء عدد من **الواجهات** المعمارية والفنية الرائعة المنحوتة. برزت على هذه **الواجهات تماثيل لأشخاص** يصعب تحديد **هويتهم** بسبب التآكل والخراب، كما نحتت صور <u>**الطيور والأسود**</u> واقفة في القمة تحمي هذا البناء.

Answer key to exercises 159

أما في وسط المدينة فيشاهد الزائر **مئات المعالم** التي **حفرها وأنشأها** الإنسان، من أضرحة ملكية إلى مدرج كبير، **وبيوت صغيرة وكبيرة وقاعات احتفالات وقنوات** ماء **وحمامات** إضافة إلى **الأسواق والبوابات**.

Translation:

The Arab Nabataeans in Southern Jordan built a great civilization during the first two centuries BC. The city of Petra, which was carved in the rocks, was among the finest things they left. They carved out temples, castles and tombs and blasted a path that led to this city with a length of two kilometers. This path is known as the *siiq*.

In Petra there are a number of finely carved architectural and artistic façades with statues of people whose identity is difficult to determine because of the corrosion and damage. There were also carved images of birds and lions standing on top to protect these structures.

As for the city center, there the visitor can see hundreds of monuments carved out and created by humans, from royal tombs to a large amphitheater, small and big houses, celebration halls, water channels, baths, as well as markets and gates.

Chapter 5

EXERCISE 1.

مكتبٌ كبيرٌ	مكتبٌ كبيرٌ أو مكتبٌ كبيرٌ
في المجلِ	في المحلِ أو في المجلِ
اشتريت شنطةً جديدةً	اشتريت شنطةً جديدةً أو اشتريت شنطةً جديدةً
مع أخي الصغيرِ	مع أخي الصغيرِ أو مع أخي الصغيرِ
بعد الحربِ الباردةِ	بعد الحربِ الباردةِ أو بعد الحربِ الباردةِ
الحديقةُ العامةُ	الحديقةُ العامةُ أو الحديقةُ العامةُ
حفظ الكلماتِ الجديدةَ	حفظ الكلماتِ الجديدةَ أو حافظ الكلماتِ الجديدةَ
قرأت المقالةَ	قرأت المقالةَ أو قرأت المقالةَ

EXERCISE 2.

١) الأستاذُ الجديدُ وطلابُه

٢) أعلنت الحكومةُ السوريةُ بيانا رسميا

٣) المتحفُ الجديدُ في أبو ظبي واسعٌ وحديثٌ.

٤) هل الرواتبُ في بلادك مناسبةٌ؟

٥) سيارتُه الجديدةُ غاليةٌ جدا.

160   *Answer key to exercises*

٦) كرةُ السلة هوايتُه المفضلةُ.

٧) الأكلُ العربي أكلٌ لذيذٌ وصحيٌّ.

٨) زوجُها سعوديٌّ.

٩) هذه القصةُ القصيرةُ الجديدةُ بديعةٌ.

١٠) يلعب الولدُ وكلبُه في الحديقة.

EXERCISE 3.

١) ذهبنا من بيتِنا القديمِ إلى شقتِنا الجديدةِ بسيارةِ ابنِ العمِ.

٢) أجابت على جميعِ الأسئلةِ.

٣) بيت العائلةِ قريب من مركزِ المدينةِ.

٤) سافر مدير الشركةِ إلى المعرضِ الدولي في العاصمةِ.

٥) يتخرج معظم الطلابِ من الجامعةِ بعد فترةٍ دراسيةٍ من أربعِ سنواتٍ.

٦) في الطابقِ الثالثِ غرفة نومٍ.

٧) مدرسة المدرسِ بعيدة عن بيتِ أسرتِه.

٨) التقى رئيس الدولةِ بنظيرِه في مؤتمرِ الدولِ العربيةِ.

٩) أكتب بقلمِ رصاصٍ في الدفترِ.

١٠) من أهمِ الثرواتِ الطبيعيةِ الموجودةِ في المنطقةِ.

EXERCISE 4.

١) اشترينا كتابًا عربيًا ودفترًا واقلامًا والألبومَ الجديدَ.

٢) في المقهى لقيتُ البنتَ اللبنانيةَ وصاحبتَها.

٣) دخل الصفَ متأخرًا.

٤) حضروا محاضرةً في الجامعة كلَ يوم.

٥) أنجزت واجباتها الكثيرةَ وبعد ذلك كتبت رسالةً.

٦) عمل أستاذًا العامَ الماضيَ.

٧) كان مريضًا ولكنه أنجز واجباتَه.

٨) نأكل الفطورَ صباحًا.

٩) أستمع إلى هذه المطربة دائمًا لأني أحب صوتَها كثيرًا.

١٠) شاهدوا المبارياتِ يومَ الأحد.

Answer key to exercises 161

EXERCISE 5.

مفرد	الإعراب والجمع السالم
متفرّج + كثير	متفرجونَ كثيرونَ
طالبة + مجتهدة	طالباتٌ مجتهداتٌ
سياسي + فاسد	سياسيونَ فاسدونَ
مع المدرّسة الجديدة	مع المدرّساتِ الجديداتِ
مع ناشط تونسي	مع ناشطينَ تونسيينَ
قابلتُ مثقفاً عراقياً	قابلتُ مثقفينَ عراقيينَ.
لاعب + مميز	لاعبونَ مميزونَ
تعمل في هذا المستشفى طبيبة مصرية.	تعمل في هذا المستشفى طبيباتٌ مصرياتٌ.
نحتفل العيد مع المسلم الاميركي.	نحتفل العيد مع المسلمين الامريكيين.
استقبلتْ تركيا لاجئاً سورياً.	استقبلتْ تركيا لاجئينَ سوريينَ.

EXERCISE 6.

الإعراب وجمع التكسير	الترجمة
اشتريتُ دَفاتراً جديدةً.	I bought new notebooks.
أشجارٌ كثيرةٌ	many trees
يسكنون في شِقَقٍ غاليةٍ.	They live in expensive apartments.
المدينة معروفة بشوارعِها النظيفةِ.	The city is known for its clean streets.
بعد أيامٍ قليلةٍ	after a few days
في هذا المنطقةِ جوامعُ قديمةٌ كثيرةٌ.	There are many old mosques in the area.

EXERCISE 7.

بعد ساعتين أو بعد ساعتين	بعد ساعتين
هناك فتاتان جميلتان أو هناك فتاتين جميلتين	هناك فتاتان جميلتان
يغضب من الوالدان أو بغضب من الوالدين	يغضب من الوالدين
استأجرت شقتان أو استأجرت شقتين	استأجرت شقتين
قرأت الكتاب مرتان أو قرأت الكتاب مرتين	قرأت الكتاب مرتين
السؤالان الصعبان أو السؤالين الصعبين	السؤالان الصعبان

162 *Answer key to exercises*

EXERCISE 8.

١) وجدتُ **السيارةَ الجديدةَ** أمام **البيتِ القديمِ**.

٢) يزور **كلُّ أفرادِ العائلةِ** هذه **المنطقةَ الجميلةَ**.

٣) ينتهى **بناءُ المكتبةِ الجديدةِ** في منتصفِ **الشهرِ المقبلِ**.

٤) تختلف **اللغةُ العربيةُ الفصحى** عن **اللغةِ العاميةِ** في بعضِ **الكلماتِ والقواعدِ**.

٥) تعرّف **الشابُ السعودي على أصحابِهِ الجُدُدِ**.

٦) صحا **محمدٌ يومَ الجمعةِ** في **الساعةِ العاشرةِ** صباحاً.

٧) استعدوا **للانتقالِ** إلى **شقةٍ جديدةٍ**.

٨) اشترتْ **كتباً كثيرةً** من **زميلِها** العربي.

٩) اشترى **الولدُ الصغيرُ الكتابَ الصغيرَ**.

EXERCISE 9.

جامعتي

جامعتي حديثةٌ وكبيرةٌ ويدرس فيها طلابٌ من أمريكا والكثيرُ من الطلابِ الأجانبِ ومن بينهم طلابٌ عربٌ. وأعرف الكثيرَ من هؤلاءِ الطلابِ العربِ. أنا طالبٌ في كليةِ الطب. هذه الكليةُ كبيرةٌ جداً. تتكون الجامعةُ من الاقسامِ العلميةِ مثل كلياتُ الفيزياءِ والكيمياءِ والزراعةِ. أما من الأقسامِ الأدبيةِ فتجد كليةَ اللغاتِ أضافةً إلى كلياتِ التربيةِ والحقوقِ والاقتصادِ وعلم الاجتماعِ. وتدرس صديقتي في معهدِ الدراساتِ الاسلاميةِ وتخصصُها هو اللغةُ العربيةُ وَآدابُها. سوف أعمل بعد الدراسةِ طبيباً في هذه المدينةِ. أما صديقتي فستسافر إلى السعوديةِ لمدةِ سنةٍ في العامِ القادمِ وستكتب رسالتَها للحصولِ على الدكتوراه.

EXERCISE 10.

١) قرأت **مقالتَهُ**.

٢) **مقالتُهُ** جيدة جدا.

٣) وجدت بعض الأخطاء في **مقالتِهِ**.

٤) هذه هي **مقالتُهُ** الأولى.

٥) كتابة **مقالتِهِ** الثانية تحتاج إلى وقت طويل.

٦) سيكتب **مقالتَهُ** الجديدة في الصيف.

٧) تُرسَل **مقالاتُهُ** إلى المجلات والجرائد.

Chapter 6

EXERCISE 1.

الزمن	الجملة
الماضي	سافرت خالتي لزيارة العائلة أمس.
المضارع	أدرس اللغة العربية منذ سنتين.
الماضي	بعد الوصول في المطار استأجرنا سيارة.
الماضي	اللاعب المشهور زين الدين زيدان سجل ثلاثة أهداف.
الماضي	لم يفهموه.
المستقبل	ستبدأ الاجازة بعد أسبوع.
المضارع	في هذه المدينة عمارات عالية تتكون من عشرة طوابق أو أكثر.
المضارع	تتأخر مغادرة الطائرة بنصف ساعة.
المستقبل	لن أنساك أبداً.
المضارع	قبل دخول البيت يدق الجرس.

EXERCISE 2.

المضارع	الماضي
نلعب كرة القدم.	لعبنا كرة القدم.
أستقبل بالضيوف في المطار.	**استقبلتُ بالضيوف في المطار.**
أجلس مع صاحبتي في المقهى.	جلستُ مع صاحبتي في المقهى.
بعد أسبوعين نسافر إلى بغداد.	**بعد أسبوعين سافرنا إلى بغداد.**
تشربون الشاي بعد الأكل.	شربتم الشاي بعد الأكل.
تتكلمين مع المدير.	**تكلمتِ مع المدير.**
ترجع البنت من الرحلة.	رجعتْ البنت من الرحلة.
ينعقد المؤتمر في الرياض.	**انعقد المؤتمر في الرياض.**
يدخّنون خارج المطعم.	دخّنوا خارج المطعم.
ترجعون إلى البيت متأخرين.	**رجعتم إلى البيت متأخرين.**
تشاهد الفيديو.	شاهدتَ الفيديو.
يأكلون طعام العشاء.	**أكلوا طعام العشاء.**
يدخل الغرفة.	دخل الغرفة.
تدرس اللغة العربية.	**درست اللغة العربية.**
تقرئين الجريدة.	قرأتِ الجريدة.
تذهب الموظفة إلى المكتب.	**ذهبتْ الموظفة إلى المكتب.**

164 *Answer key to exercises*

EXERCISE 3.

الوزن	الماضي	المضارع	المصدر	الترجمة
VI	تَعامَلَ	يَتعامَل	التَعامُل	to cooperate
VIII	اِشْتَرَكَ	يَشْتَرِك	الاِشْتِراك	to participate
IV	أَرْسَلَ	يُرْسِل	الإرْسال	to send
V	تَفَرَّجَ	يَتَفَرَّج	التفرُّج	to watch
II	حَقَّقَ	يُحَقِّق	التَحْقيق	to analyze
III	شاهَدَ	يُشاهِد	المُشاهَدة	to see
I	قَرَأَ	يَقْرَأ	القِراءة	to read
X	اِسْتَثْمَرَ	يَسْتَثْمِر	الاِسْتِثْمار	to invest
VII	اِنْعَقَدَ	يَنْعَقِد	الاِنْعِقاد	to hold

EXERCISE 4.

الفعل الضعيف	صواب أو خطأ
خافتُ البنت من العاصفة.	صواب
باعنا بيتنا.	خطأ
نشترى الخضار من السوق.	صواب
سألته عن القضية.	صواب
أأكل العشاء في المطعم.	خطأ
مشتُ ساعات طويلة.	خطأ
كانا أنا وأصحابي سعداء.	خطأ
يصلون إلى المطار.	صواب
تنتهي المباراة في الساعة الخامسة.	صواب
هل أرادتم الخروج؟	خطأ

EXERCISE 5.

الفعل الضعيف الماضي - هو/هي	الفعل الضعيف الماضي - أنا
زار الرئيس المنطقة الشمالية.	زرتُ المنطقة الشمالية.
عادت من النادي متأخرة.	عُدتُ من النادي متأخرة.
كان جوعان جدا.	كُنتُ جوعان جداً.
قالت له إنها مرتاحة.	قُلتُ له إنني مرتاحة.
انتهى من الواجبات.	انتهيتُ من الواجبات.
باعت ملابس شتوية.	بِعتُ ملابس شتوية.

Answer key to exercises   165

الفعل الضعيف الماضي - أنا	الفعل الضعيف الماضي - هو/هي
وصلتُ مساء الأمس.	وصل صديقي مساء الأمس.
تمنيتُ أن أكون مثلها.	تمنى أن يكون مثلها.
اشتريتُ تذكرتين للمباراة.	اشترى تذكرتين للمباراة.
أردتُ البقاء في البيت.	أرادت البقاء في البيت.
أعطيته المفتاح.	أعطته المفتاح.

EXERCISE 6.

(١)   الوالدان **يسكنان** في نفس البيت.

(٢)   أنا وأخي **سافرا** لزيارة جدنا أمس.

(٣)   الرئيسان السوري والايراني **يناقشان** قضايا مهمة في زيارة عمل.

(٤)   علمتُ بأن أخي خالد وصديقتي مريم **تزوجا** قبل أسبوع.

(٥)   الفريقان الأهلي والشباب **يشاركان** في بطولة كأس الأبطال.

(٦)   يا سليمان وعلي، هل **ساعدتما** عم حسين في شغل المحل؟

(٧)   غدا، أنتما **تزوران** الجيران.

(٨)   الطالبتان **نجحا** في التوجيهي.

EXERCISE 7.

I love you.	أحبك.
He hates me.	يكرهني.
Can you help me please?	هل يمكنك أن تساعدني من فضلك؟
They don't understand us.	لا يفهموننا.
She took it from me.	أخذته منّي.
He left her and her family.	تركها وأسرتها.
This suits me very well.	هذا يناسبني كثيرا.
I bought it for only 10 Riyal.	اشتريته بعشرة ريالات فقط.
Please give me your phone number.	لو سمحت، أعطني رقم تليفونك.
He saw her last night.	شاهدها الليلة الماضية.

166 *Answer key to exercises*

EXERCISE 8.

ضمير الملك أو النصب؟	الجملة بالضمير
الملك	يعيش مع أسرته.
الملك	يساعد أخته بالواجب.
النصب	يساعدها كثيرا.
النصب	لا يحبونه.
النصب	قابلتهم في المدينة.
النصب	استقبلني في المطار.
الملك	خذ راحتك.
الملك	أريد مساعدتكم.
النصب	هل يمكنكم أن تساعدوني؟
النصب	اشتريته من السوق.

EXERCISE 9.

أنا آسف ولكني لا أستطيع الخروج معكم.	أنا آسف ولكني لا أستطيع أن أخرج معكم.
شجعني والدي على الالتحاق بالجيش.	**شجعني والدي على أن ألتحق بالجيش.**
يمكنك دفع الحساب غدا.	يمكنك أن تدفع الحساب غدا.
قررنا البقاء في هذه المنطقة.	**قررنا أن نبقى في هذه المنطقة.**
أتمنى الانتقال إلى مدينة بعيدة.	أتمنى أن أنتقل إلى مدينة بعيدة.
أراد الشعب ارحال الرئيس الظالم.	**أراد الشعب أن يرحل الرئيس الظالم.**
اسمح لي تقديم نفسي.	إسمح لي أن أقدم نفسي.
طلبتُ منهم العودة إلى البيت فوراً.	**طلبت منهم أن يعودوا إلى البيت فورا.**
يجب عليّ الدراسة والحفظ الكثير قبل التخرج من الجامعة.	يجب عليّ أن أدرس وأحفظ كثيراً قبل أن أتخرج من الجامعة.

EXERCISE 10.

Get up!	يقوم	قُم	Come back!	يرجع	إِرْجَع
Eat!	يأكل	كُل	Be quiet!	يسكت	أُسكُت
Sit!	يجلس	إِجْلِس	Watch!	يشاهد	شاهِد
Ask!	يسأل	إِسأَل	Play!	يلعب	إلْعُب
Write!	يكتب	أُكْتُب	Grab!	يمسك	أُمْسِك

Answer key to exercises 167

EXERCISE 11.

هو رجل طويل.	**هو ليس رجل طويل.**
نريد أن نزور الأردن في الصيف.	**لا نريد أن نزور الأردن في الصيف.**
أغضب منك.	**لا أغضب منك.**
اليوم عندنا واجبات كثيرة.	**اليوم ما / ليس عندنا واجبات كثيرة.**
كان الامتحان صعباً جدا.	**ما كان / لم يكن الامتحان صعباً جدا.**
هل فهمتم هذا السؤال؟	**ما فهمنا / لم نفهمْ هذا السؤال.**
يشترك كل الطلاب في مباراة كرة القدم.	**لا يشترك كل الطلاب في مباراة كرة القدم.**
يملك الناس في مصر الحرية.	**لا يملك الناس في مصر الحرية.**
هل يمكنني أن أخرج مع أصدقائي في الليل؟	**لا، لا يمكنك أن تخرج مع أصدقائك في الليل.**
سأخرج من الجامعة بعد هذا الفصل.	**لن أتخرجَ من الجامعة بعد هذا الفصل.**
هل عندك وقت بعد الظهر؟	**لا، ما / ليس عندي وقت بعد الظهر.**
كانت البنت مشغولة بواجباتها.	**ما كانت / لم تكن البنت مشغولة بواجباتها.**
في هذه المدينة شوارع كثيرة.	**ليست في هذه المدينة شوارع كثيرة.**

EXERCISE 12.

إقرأ الجملة!	**لا تقرأ الجملة!**
خذي الشنطة!	**لا تأخذي الشنطة!**
أدخلوا الغرفة!	**لا تدخلوا الغرفة!**
إمش إلى هناك!	**لا تمشي إلى هناك!**
أكتب لي!	**لا تكتب لي!**
إشربي القهوة!	**لا تشربي القهوة!**
كرروا الكلمات!	**لا تكرروا الكلمات!**
أمسك الصورة!	**لا تمسك الصورة!**
إذهب إلى هذا المكان!	**لا تذهب إلى هذا المكان!**
سافروا معهم!	**لا تسافروا معهم!**

EXERCISE 13.

أقام الوزير حفلة عشاء.	**أُقيمتْ حفلة عشاء.**
غيّر الرئيس البرنامج.	**غُيِّرَ البرنامج.**
شاهدنا الطلاب أمام الجامعة.	**شوهِدَ الطلاب أمام الجامعة.**
يسلّم أحمد الكتاب غداً.	**يُسَلَّم الكتاب غداً.**
كتب الكاتب الكتاب.	**كُتِبَ الكتاب.**

168 *Answer key to exercises*

منع الوالد التدخين.	مُنِعَ التدخين.
يعتبر الطلاب الدرس سهلاً.	يُعْتَبَر الدرس سهلاً.
طبخت الوالدة الطعام للإفطار.	طُبِخَت الطعام للإفطار.

EXERCISE 14.

الوزن	الشخص	الزمن	الفعل	
٣	أنا	الماضي	قابلتُ	(١
١	هو	المضارع	يسكن	(٢
١	هو	الماضي	جاء	(٣
١	نحن	الماضي	ذهبنا	(٤
١	هو	الماضي	أكل	(٥
١	أنا	الماضي	أكلتُ	(٦
١	هو	الماضي	كان	(٧
١	نحن	الماضي	شربنا	(٨
٢	نحن	الماضي	دخّننا	(٩
٨	نحن	الماضي	استمعنا	(١٠
٥	هي	الماضي	تكلمتْ	(١١
١	هو	الماضي	جاء	(١٢
١	هو	الماضي	حدث	(١٣
١	هو	الماضي	شرح	(١٤
١	هي	الماضي	فرضتْ	(١٥
١	هم	الماضي	زالوا	(١٦
١	هم	المضارع	يعيشون	(١٧
٣	هو	الماضي	سافر	(١٨
١	نحن	الماضي	لقينا	(١٩
١	أنا	المستقبل	سأرجع	(٢٠
١٠	هو	الماضي	استأجر	(٢١
١	هو	المضارع	يجب	(٢٢
١	نحن	المضارع	نحكي	(٢٣
١	أنا	الماضي	سمعتُ	(٢٤
١	هو	الماضي	وجد	(٢٥
١	هي	الماضي	حصلتْ	(٢٦
١	هي	المضارع	تبحث	(٢٧
٤	أنا	المضارع	أريد	(٢٨
٣	أنا	المضارع	أساعد	(٢٩

Translation:

Last week I met my friend Ridwan, who lives in Syria, but came to visit me. We went to a small restaurant for dinner where Ridwan ate some kebab and I ate soup and salad. The food was not good. After dinner we drank tea and had a cigarette. We listened to the news and the announcer talked about the war in Syria. Finally the time came to talk about what had happened there over the past months. He explained to me that his family was forced to flee from the village. They still live in a refugee camp. But he and his sister traveled to Lebanon, where we met again. Today I will go back again to his apartment, which he rented for a week, in order to talk about many things. I heard that he found a new job. As for his sister, who obtained a BA in education, she is also looking for a job. I want to help her with this search.

Chapter 7

EXERCISE 1.

The economic situation in Europe is difficult.	الوضع الاقتصادي في أوروبا صعب.
My family is very poor.	**عائلتي فقيرة جدا.**
They live next to the mosque.	هم يسكنون جنب المسجد.
I have only one sister.	**لي أخت واحدة فقط.**
Lebanese food is delicious.	الأكل اللبناني لذيذ جداً.
Today the weather is sunny and warm.	**الجو مشمس وحار اليوم.**
She has a daughter in kindergarten.	لها بنت في الروضة.
Do you have time this afternoon?	**هل عندك وقت بعد الظهر؟**
Do you have a computer at home?	هل عندك كمبيوتر في البيت؟
The post office is near the train station.	**مكتب البريد قريب من المحطة.**
The house has three storeys.	في المنزل ثلاثة طوابق.
My friends are from Sudan.	**أصحابي من السودان.**
The new president is unpopular with the people.	الرئيس الجديد غير محبوب لدى الجماهير.
Do you have a question?	**هل عندك سؤال؟**
The weather in the mountains is cold in the winter.	الجو في الجبال بارد في الشتاء.
Cairo is an old and beautiful city.	**القاهرة مدينة قديمة وجميلة.**
She is sick.	هي مريضة.
We have a farm in the countryside.	**عندنا مزرعة في الريف.**
My dad works in trade.	والدي يعمل في التجارة.
Studying Arabic is hard!	**دراسة اللغة العربية صعبة.**

170 *Answer key to exercises*

EXERCISE 2.

موظف شركة في والدي آرامكو السعودية في.	والدي موظف في شركة آرامكو في السعودية.
كل ساعات يعمل يوم طويلة.	يعمل ساعات طويلة كل يوم.
وقت عائلة ليس مع لديه.	ليس لديه وقت مع العائلة.
للسباحة كلنا نذهب البحر إلى.	كلنا نذهب إلى البحر للسباحة.
الكُرة يلعب إخوتي وأخواتي مع.	يلعب إخوتي وأخواتي مع الكُرة.
غروب البيت نعود إلى الشمس بعد.	نعود إلى البيت بعد غروب الشمس.
الدوام في الشركة في يبدأ الصباح غدا.	يبدأ الدوام في الشركة في الصباح غدا.
المدرسة الأولاد يدرس في.	يدرس الأولاد في المدرسة.

EXERCISE 3.

الجملة الاسمية	الجملة الفعلية
الطالبات يشربن الشاي بعد المحاضرات.	تشرب الطالبات الشاي بعد المحاضرات.
الشباب التحقوا في الجيش.	التحق الشباب في الجيش.
قوات الاحتلال ترفع حصارها على الأقصى.	ترفع قوات الاحتلال حصارها على الأقصى.
شركة كانون تطور عدسة سينمائية جديدة.	تطور شكرة كانون عدسة سينمائية جديدة.
الفرق العربية تودع أبطال آسيا.	تودع الفرق العربية أبطال آسيا.
إنتر وميونخ تعادلا في كأس الأبطال.	تعادل إنتر وميونج في كأس الأبطال.
المشاكل المالية تقلل القدرة على التفكير.	تقلل المشاكل المالية القدرة على التفكير.
جميع أندية الطلبة شاركت في مهرجان الجامعة.	شاركت جميع أندية الطلبة في مهرجان الجامعة.
نواب مجلس الشورى عقدوا اجتماعا.	عقد نواب مجلس الشورى اجتماعا.
الأولاد لم يسافروا مع والديهم.	لم يسافر الأولاد مع والديهم.
الطلاب استمعوا إلى محاضرة الأستاذ.	استمع الطلاب إلى محاضرة الأستاذ.
الجامعات الأوربية توفر منحا للطلاب الأجانب.	توفر الجامعات الأوربية منحا للطلاب الأجانب.
العثمانيون انسحبوا من بغداد عام ١٩١٧.	انسحب العثمانيون من بغداد عام ١٩١٧.
طلاب كثيرون يتغيبون عن دراساتهم بسبب الجو المثلج.	يتغيب طلاب كثيرون عن دراساتهم بسبب الجو المثلج.

الجملة الفعلية	الجملة الاسمية
تستخدم القوات السورية سلاح الحرمان من الصحة.	القوات السورية تستخدم سلاح الحرمان من الصحة.
اكتمل بناء جامع القرويين في مدينة فاس عام ٨٥٩.	بناء جامع القرويين في مدينة فاس اكتمل عام ٨٥٩.

EXERCISE 4.

عندما رجعتُ إلى المنزل كان العشاء جاهزاً.

عندما كنت في القاهرة زرت الأهرام.

عندما وصلوا إلى المسرح ذهبوا إلى مقاعدهم فوراً.

عندما سمعتُ الخبر الأبيض كانت سعيدة جداً.

عندما سمعتُ خبر وفاة عمي كنتُ حزيناً وبكيتُ كثيراً.

عندما يشاهد الزوج التلفزيون تطبخ الزوجة العشاء.

عندما أسهر مع الأصحاب أصحو متأخراً في الصباح الثاني.

عندما دق الباب فتح الباب.

EXERCISE 5.

(١) ألغينا رحلتنا إلى بيروت بسبب الأحداث بسوريا.

(٢) أحبك لأنك أجمل فتاة في العالم.

(٣) كل شيء يحدث بسبب.

(٤) ذهبنا إلى الملعب من أجل مشاهدة المباراة.

(٥) أنا زعلان جدا لأن فريقي خسر هذه المباراة المهمة.

(٦) بقيت في البيت لأقضي وقتا طيبا مع عائلتي.

(٧) فشل في الامتحان بسبب الأخطاء الكثيرة.

(٨) لم يحضر الحفلة لأنه كان مريضاً.

EXERCISE 6.

No answer is provided for this exercise.

EXERCISE 7.

(١) زرت الصديق الذي تعرفتُ عليه منذ شهر.

(٢) هم أصحاب جاؤوا من السعودية.

(٣) حكيت مع جاري الذي يسكن بجاني.

(٤) سمعت أغنية لم أسمعها منذ طفولتي.

(٥) هذه هي الأستاذة التي فشلتُ الامتحان معها.

172 Answer key to exercises

٦) لي أخت اسمها يسرى.

٧) ذكرتُ هذا من كتاب قرأتُه الأسبوع الماضي.

٨) كانت السيارة **التي** اشتريتها أمس غالية جدا.

٩) ما هو احسن فلم شاهدته؟

١٠) أعرف مكاناً أريد أن أذهب إليه.

١١) رحب الرئيس بالضيوف **الذين** حضروا الاجتماع.

١٢) تعرفت على لاعبين جاؤوا من كل أنحاء العالم.

EXERCISE 8.

انجليزي	عربي
We invited all the relatives except for the wife of Uncle Husayn.	دعونا كل الأقارب إلا زوجة عمي حسين.
I only have one question.	**ما عندي سؤال إلا واحد.**
He only scored two goals in the game.	لم يسجل في المباريات إلا هدفين.
Nobody said anything except for the president.	**لم يتكلم أحد إلا الرئيس.**
I don't like any Arabic food except for Kunaafa.	لا أحب الأكل العربي إلا الكنافة.
It is 5:45 p.m.	**الساعة السادسة إلا الربع.**
He only came back home after two years.	لم يعد الى الوطن إلا بعد سنتين.
Only they will know.	**لا أحد يعرف الا هم.**
I confess that there is no other woman but you. (Nizar Qabbani)	أشهد أن لا امرأة إلا أنت. (نزار قباني)
I am not afraid of any animals except for snakes.	**لا أخاف من الحيوانات إلا الحيات.**

EXERCISE 9.

جملة الحال بالإنجليزي	جملة الحال بالعربي
She left him crying.	**تركته باكية.**
He came to Cairo when he was young.	جاء إلى القاهرة صغيراً.
The girl smiles while reading his email.	**تبتسم البنت وتقرأ الايميل منه.**
He was late for his meeting when he entered the office.	دخل المكتب متأخراً لموعده.
The old man sat in the café drinking his coffee.	**جلس الشيخ في المقهى ويشرب القهوة.**
Don't drink the water when it is cold.	لا تشرب الماء بارداً!

جملة الحال بالعربي	جملة الحال بالإنجليزي
استمعوا إلى المحاضرة ولا يقولون كلمة.	They listened to the lecture without saying a word.
سافر إلى الصين نائماً طول الرحلة.	**When he traveled to China he slept the entire trip.**
كتب هذه القصيدة وقد فكّر عن الوطن.	He wrote this poem while thinking about his homeland.
تركتُ اليمن وأنا طفلة.	**I left Yemen as a young child.**

EXERCISE 10.

بكم كيلو بندورة؟	كيلو بندورة بعشرين قرش.
مع من تسكن؟	أسكن مع أخي واثنين من أصحابي.
هل استمتعت به؟	نعم، استمتعتُ به كثيراً.
إلى أين تسافر هذا الصيف؟	نسافر إلى تونس هذا الصيف.
أين أطول بناية؟	أطول بناية في دبي.
كم طولها؟	طولها كيلو ونصف تقريباً.
من أين اشتريته؟	اشتريتُه من السوق.
أين عشت؟	عشت في مدينة دمشق.
كم الساعة الآن؟	الآن الساعة الواحدة تماماً.
كم عمرك؟	عمري ثلاثين سنة.
كم رجلاً في الغرفة؟	في الغرفة أربعة رجال فقط.
هل لك أخ؟	لا، ليس لي أخ.
هل سمعتَ الخبر؟	لم أسمع الخبر.
لماذا لم يحضر؟	لأنه كان مريضاً.
ماذا درستم في الصف أمس؟	درسنا القواعد في الصف أمس.
متى عيد ميلادك؟	عيد ميلادي في أول من سبتمبر.
متى ولدت؟	ولدت في سنة ١٩٨٣.
من هي البنت التي كانت معك في النادي؟	البنت التي كانت معي في النادي هي بنت عمي.
هل عندك وقت؟	لا، ما عندي وقت.
هل تظن أنه صحيح؟	لا، أظن أنه خطأ.
ماذا تريد؟	لا أريد أي شيء.

Chapter 8

EXERCISE 1.

السؤال	الجواب
٤ زائد ٨ يساوي كم؟	١٢ / اثنا عشر
٢٠ ناقص ١٣ يساوي كم؟	٧ / سبعة
٥٥ على ١١ يساوي كم؟	٥ / خمسة
٧ في ٩ يساوي كم؟	٦٣ / ثلاثة وستون
في ٣ ساعات كم دقيقة؟	١٨٠ / مائة وثمانون
اشتريت الكتاب بستة ريالات ونصف ودفعت بعشرة ريالات. كم الباقي؟	ثلاثة ريالات ونصف
٣٣ + ٢٩ - ٥ = ؟	٥٧ / سبعة وخمسون
واحد دولار يساوي ٣٫٧٥ ريال سعودي. كم يساوي واحد ريال بالدولار؟	٢٧ / سبعة وعشرون سنتاً
زرت قطر والبحرين وعمان. كم دولة عربية تبقى قبل أن أزور كلها؟	تبقى ٢١ / إحدى وعشرون دولة عربية.
كم ساعة تدرس اللغة العربية كل يوم؟	أدرس عربي ساعتين كل يوم.

EXERCISE 2.

٨ سيارة / ثماني سيارات	١١ شهر / احد عشر شهرا	٥ صلاة / خمس صلوات
٣ بيت / ثلاثة بيوت	١٠ نقطة / عشر نقط	٢٢ سنة / اثنتان وعشرون سنة
١٢ مدينة / اثنتا عشرة مدينة	١١٢ غرفة / مئة واثنتا عشرة غرفة	٢٠٦٩ نسخة / ألفان وتسع وستون نسخة
٢ قلم / قلمان	٤٥ طالبة / خمس وأربعون طالبة	١٢٥٠٩ طفل / اثنا عشر الف وخمسمئة وتسعة أطفال
٢١ شخص / واحد وعشرون شخصا	٢٠٢ صفحة / مئتا صفحة وصفحتان	٣٠ أسبوع / ثلاثون أسبوعا
٩٩٩ ريال / تسعمئة وتسعة وتسعون ريالا	١ حبة / حبة واحدة	١٠٠١ ليلة / ألف ليلة وليلة

Answer key to exercises 175

EXERCISE 3.

انجليزي	عربي	انجليزي	عربي
the 1st place	المكان الأول	the 4th year	السنة الرابعة
the 5th street	الشارع الخامس	in the 21st century	في القرن الحادي والعشرين
the 26th floor	الطابق السادس والعشرون	the 7th goal	الهدف السابع
the 7th day of the week	اليوم السابع في الأسبوع	the 2nd entrance	المدخل الثاني
for the 100th time	للمرة المائة	the first class degree	الدرجة الأولى

EXERCISE 4.

عشرون طابقا	الطابق العشرون	اليوم الثالث	ثلاثة أيام
ثلاثة أيام	اليوم الثالث	الأسبوع الثاني	أسبوعان
ثماني سنوات	السنة الثامنة	الشهر الخامس	خمسة شهور
تسعة عشر قرنا	القرن التاسع عشر	السنة التاسعة	تسع سنوات
دقيقة واحدة	الدقيقة الأولى	الساعة الثانية عشرة	اثنتا عشرة ساعة
عشر دورات	الدورة العاشرة	المرة المائة	مائة مرة
ساعة واحدة	الساعة الواحدة	الهدف الأول	هدف واحد
خمس مدارس	المدرسة الخامسة	القرن الرابع عشر	أربعة عشر قرناً

EXERCISE 5.

(١) هذا اليوم التاسع عشر في شهر شباط.

(٢) أمس كان خمسة طلاب واثنتا عشرة طالبة في الصف.

(٣) فاز الفريق للمرة الأولى.

(٤) تغادر الطائرة في الساعة الحادية عشرة وخمس وعشرين دقيقة.

(٥) اشترت أمي ستة وعشرين أشياء مفيدة.

(٦) استمع أكثر من مائتي طالب إلى المحاضرة.

(٧) شاركت اثنتان وثلاثون دولة في مباريات كأس العالم.

(٨) نعيش في القرن الحادي والعشرين.

EXERCISE 6.

أيار	الشهر الخامس في المشرق
ذو الحجة	الشهر الهجري الثاني عشر
رمضان	الشهر الهجري التاسع
كانون الثاني	الشهر الأول في المشرق

176 Answer key to exercises

ديسمبر	الشهر الآخر في المغرب
آب	**الشهر الثامن في المشرق**
شباط	الشهر الهجري الثاني
مارس	**الشهر الثالث في المغرب**
نيسان	الشهر الرابع في المشرق
ربيع الأول	**الشهر الهجري الثالث**

EXERCISE 7.

midnight, 12:00 a.m.	في الساعة الثانية عشرة مساءً
11:45 a.m.	**في الساعة الثانية عشرة إلا الربع**
4:20	في الساعة الرابعة والثلث
6:05 p.m.	**في الساعة السادسة وخمس دقائق مساءً**
5:50	في الساعة السادسة إلا عشر دقائق
exactly 12:15	**في الساعة الثانية عشرة والربع تماماً**
1:30	في الساعة الواحدة والنصف
3:50 in the afternoon	**في الساعة الرابعة إلا عشر دقائق عصراً**
8:25	في الساعة الثامنة وخمس وعشرين دقيقة
7:12 a.m.	**في الساعة السابعة واثنتي عشرة دقيقة صباحاً**

on the first day of March 2012 في اليوم الأول من آذار عام ألفين واثني عشر

My father passed away on Jan. 31, 1972.

توفي والدي في الأول من كانون الثاني عام ألف وتسعمئة واثنين وسبعين.

ولدت في العشرين من شباط سنة ألف وتسعمائة وأربع وسبعين.
I was born on the 20th of February 1974.

ولدت في سنة ألف وثلاثمئة وتسع وثمانين هجري. I was born in 1389 H.

أصدر هذا الكتاب في سنة مائتين وثلاث وأربعين هـ.

This book was published in 243 AH.

Sarah graduated from high school in 1994.

تخرجت سارة من المدرسة الثانوية سنة ألف وتسعمئة وأربع وتسعين.

في عام ألفين واثني عشر الميلادي الموافق عام ألف وأربعمائة وثلاثة وثلاثين الهجري
in the year 2012 AD/1433 AH

The film opened on March 1, 2003.

فتح الفلم في الأول من مارس (آذار) سنة ألفين وثلاث.

توفي الشيخ زايد في الثاني من نوفمبر عام ألفين وأربعة.

Shaykh Zayid died on November 2nd, 2004.

World War II ended on May 8, 1945.

انتهت الحرب العالمية الثانية في الثامن من مايو (أيار) سنة ألف وتسعمئة وخمس وأربعين.

EXERCISE 8.

the four rightly guided caliphs	الخلفاء الراشدون الأربعة
the five pillars of Islam	أركان الإسلام الخمسة
two million pilgrims	مليونا حجي
He lives in room 402.	يسكن في غرفة أربعمئة وإثنين.
I have three brothers and two sisters.	لي ثلاثة إخوة وأختان.

I was born on December 22, 1981.

ولدتُ في الثاني والعشرين من ديسمبر عام ألف وتسعمئة وواحد وثمانين.

The shop opens at 9:30 a.m. and closes at 10:45 p.m.

يفتح المحل في الساعة التاسعة والنصف صباحاً ويغلق في الساعة الحادية عشرة إلا الربع مساءً.

The party starts at 4:15 p.m.   تبدأ الحفلة في الساعة الرابعة والربع مساءً.

A barrel of oil costs $103.50.   برميل النفط بمئة وثلاثة دولارات وخمسين سنتاً.

A gallon of gasoline costs $3.99.

غلون البنزين بثلاثة دولارات وتسعة وتسعين سنتاً.

This week I went to the gym three times.

هذا الاسبوع ذهبت إلى الصالة الرياضية ثلاث مرات.

My dad told me to come home at exactly 8:00 p.m.

طلب أبي متّي أن أعود إلى البيت في الساعة الثامنة تماماً.

Today is February 9, 2012.   اليوم التاسع من فبراير / شباط عام ألفين واثني عشر.

EXERCISE 9.

I have four children.   لي أربعة أولاد.

I am a third year student.   أنا طالب في السنة الثالثة.

كنت اشتغل في هذه الشركة لمدة سنتين.

I was working at this company for two years.

غادرت الطائرة في الساعة الخامسة صباحاً.

The plane departed at five in the morning.

I was born in 1991.   ولدت في عام ألف وتسعمائة وواحد وتسعين.

ثمانية قتلى وعشرات من الجرحى في انفجار انتحاري ببغداد.

Eight killed and dozens wounded in a suicide attack in Baghdad.

178 *Answer key to exercises*

فاز الأهلي على الشباب بثلاثة أهداف مقابل هدفين.

Al-Ahli won over al-Shabab three goals to two.

We meet at 6:25.   نلتقي في الساعة السادسة وخمس وعشرين دقيقة.

درجة الحرارة في القاهرة اليوم سبع وثلاثون درجة والرطوبة خمسة وثمانون بالمائة.

The temperature in Cairo today is 37 degrees and the humidity is 85%.

الكتاب بتسعة عشر دولارا وتسعة وتسعين سنتا فقط!

The book costs only 10 dollars and 99 cents.

EXERCISE 10.

ولدتُ في **الخامس عشر** من شهر تشرين **الثاني** عام **ألف وتسعمئة ثلاثة وثمانين** في مدينة بيروت. لي **أربعة** إخوة وأخت. دخلتُ المدرسة الابتدائية في **ستة** من عمري. درستُ فيها لمدة **أربع** سنوات. في عام **ألف وتسعمئة وتسعين** تخرجتُ من المدرسة الثانوية. في الجامعة درستُ الهندسة لمدة **أربع** سنوات واللغة الفرنسية لمدة **سنتين**. في عام **ألف وتسعمئة وأربعة وتسعين** سافرتُ إلى كندا وبقيتُ فيها **عشرة** أسابيع. في الأسبوع **الأول** وجدتُ وظيفة مناسبة في شركة تجارية وقررتُ البقاء فيها **ستة** أشهر على الأقل ولكن بالصراحة بقيتُ هناك فترة قصيرة فقط يعني أقل من **أربعة** أسابيع ثم رجعتُ إلى الوطن بسبب زواجي. زوجتي عمرها **اثنتان وعشرون** سنة وهي تعمل مترجمة في نفس الشركة التجارية. هي تتكلم **خمس** لغات. اللغة **السادسة** التي تدرسها الآن هي اللغة الصينية. نعمل في نفس البناية ومكتبها في الطابق **الثالث والعشرين** ومكتبي في الطابق **الحادي عشر**. كل يوم نلتقي **ثلاث** مرات وبعد نهاية الدوام نعود إلى البيت في الساعة **الخامسة وخمس وأربعين** دقيقة.

Chapter 9

EXERCISE 1.

Love makes you blind.	الحب أعمى	The Cold War	الحرب الباردة
weapons of mass destruction (WMD)	أسلحة الدمار الشامل	Walls have ears.	الجدران لها آذان
Thanksgiving	عيد الشكر	crocodile tears	دموع التماسيح

EXERCISE 2.

sandwich	ساندويتش	computer	كمبيوتر
tennis	التنس	democracy	ديموقراطية
technology	تكنولوجية	cinema	سينما
telephone	تليفون	petroleum (oil)	بترول

Answer key to exercises 179

EXERCISE 3.

He who is afraid of the sparrow will never plant.   من خاف العصفور ما زرع

عصفور باليد أحسن من اثنين في السجرة
A bird in the hand is worth two in the bush.

Hitting two birds with one stone.   يضرب عصفورين بحجر واحد

The white penny will save the black day.   القرش الأبيض ينفع في اليوم الأسود

He who searches will find.   من جدَّ وَجَد

A boy is a boy even if he becomes the town's judge.   الولد ولد لو صار قاضي البلد

Your nose is a part of you, even if it is crooked.   أنفك منك ولو كان أجُدع

If you are a liar, you had better be a good one.   إن كنتَ كذوباً فكُن ذكوراً

EXERCISE 4.

Red Marrakesh   مراكش الحمراء

Green Tunis   تونس الخضراء

White Algiers   الجزائر البيضاء

Gray Aleppo   حلب الشهباء

the Black Sea   البحر الأسود

white (good) news   خبر أبيض

the City of Blue (al-Zarqa in Jordan)   مدينة الزرقاء

the gold medal   الميدالية الذهبية

the Qatari national team – the Maroons   منتخب قطر الوطني – العنابي

the Ivory Coast   ساحل العاج

EXERCISE 5.

دائماً	أخي الصغير جوعان	
مطلقاً	يرفضون الاتفاق	
جيداً	أعرفه	
ليلاً و نهاراً	درسنا للتوجيهات	
سنوياً	يجتمع الخبراء	
كثيراً	أحبها	
بطيئاً	يعمل الموظف	
عادةً	أصحو في الساعة ٦	

180 *Answer key to exercises*

EXERCISE 6.

صواب	خطأ
يقرأ الجريدة في الصباح.	يقرأ في صباحا الجريدة.
في الصيف نسافر إلى البحر دائماً.	في صيف نسافر دائما الى البحر.
لا يحبون البقلاوة كثيراً.	لا يحبون البقلاوة جداً.
تقرأ أختي القصص القصيرة كثيراً.	كثير أختي القصص القصيرة يقرأ.
ينام في المساء بسرعة.	في المساءً ينام بسريعاً.
أعرف كلمات عربية كثيرة.	أعرف كلمات عربيات كثيرات.
تعمل أختي قريباً من بيتها.	قريب من بيتها أختي تعمل.
في الصباح أنا جوعان جداً.	في صباحاً أنا كثير جوعان.

EXERCISE 7.

It is necessary to	من اللازم أنْ
It was wrong to	كان من الخاطئ أنْ
It is strange to	من الغريب أنْ
It is worth mentioning that	من الجدير بالذكر أنْ
It was nice to	كان من اللطيف أنْ
It wasn't hard to	ما كان من الصعب أنْ
It is important to	من المهم أنْ
It is impossible to	من المستحيل أنْ

EXERCISE 8.

(١)   يريد **أنْ** يذهب إلى هناك.

(٢)   يمكنني **أنْ** أخرج معكم.

(٣)   ظننت **أنَّ** الفلم كان طويلاً ومملاً.

(٤)   تقول ريمة **إنَّها** لا تحضر الحفلة.

(٥)   قرأنا في الجريدة **أنَّ** الاقتصاد أحسن من السنة الماضية.

(٦)   استطاع الجيش **أنْ** يدخل هذه المنطقة.

(٧)   سمعوا في الأخبار **أنَّ** الرئيس استقال.

(٨)   شعرت البنت **بأنَّها** ليست جميلة مثل صاحباتها.

EXERCISE 9.

I invited several friends to the party.	دعوتُ عدة أصدقاء للحفلة.
Last week I wrote some of my friends.	كتبتُ بعض أصدقائي الأسبوع الماضي.

Answer key to exercises 181

My mom bought the same dress.	إِشترتْ أمي نفس الفستان.
We went to the store several times.	ذهبنا إلى المحل عدة مرات.
I spent the entire day cleaning my room.	قضيتُ كل اليوم بتنظيف غرفتي.
We arrived at our hotel after several hours.	وصلنا إلى فندقنا بعد عدة ساعات.
All of the guests came to the party.	جاء كل الضيوف إلى الحفلة.
Some people don't like this book.	لا يحب بعض الناس هذا الكتاب.

During the summer break every day was beautiful.

في العطلة الصيفية كانتْ كل الأيام جميلة.

One of the guys was kind.	كان أحد الشباب لطيفاً.
All of them were there.	كان كلهم هناك.
She completed the project herself.	انجزتْ المشروع بنفسها.

The president talked to the foreign minister as well as the finance minister.

تكلم الرئيس مع كل من وزير الخارجية ووزير المالية.

I read the entire book.	قرأتُ الكتاب كله.
Did you do that by yourself?	هل فعلتَ ذلك بنفسك؟
Every day I get up at 6 a.m.	أصحو كل يوم في الساعة السادسة.
Most of my relatives live in Jordan.	يعيش معظم أقاربي في الأردن.
Yesterday I met one of them.	قابلتُ أحد منهم أمس.
Do you have everything?	هل عندكَ كل شيء؟
They ate some of the food.	أكلوا بعض الطعام.

EXERCISE 10.

You are slow like a turtle.	أنت بطئ كالسُلَحْفاة.
I am not like you.	أنا لستُ مثلك.
The Ferrari is as fast as the wind.	سيارة فيراري سريعة كالريح.
As you all know this is not right.	كما تعرفون هذا ليس صحيح.
Ahmad is a doctor like his dad.	أحمد طبيب مثل والدِهِ.
You behave like a little boy.	تتصرف كأنك ولد صغير.
I am a student like him.	أنا طالب مثلَهُ.
As you asked for.	كما طلبت.

182 *Answer key to exercises*

EXERCISE 11.

١) شكرا **لعدم** التدخين في الغرفة.

٢) يعمل مع شركة **غير** حكومية.

٣) ارتكب الخطأ **غير** مقصود.

٤) معهد تعليم اللغة العربية **لغير** الناطقين بها.

٥) وقع الطرفان معاهدة **عدم** الاعتداء.

٦) يعاني اللاجئون من **عدم** وجود الأمن والطعام.

٧) **عدم** قدرة الطلاب على دفع الأقساط

٨) صوتها **غير** واضح.

EXERCISE 12.

إِنجليزي	عربي
I worked hard until I finished all my tasks.	بذلتُ جهداً كبيراً حتى أنجزتُ واجباتي كلها.
I refuse dictatorship even under the pretext of religion.	أرفض الدكتاتورية حتى ولو على أساس ديني.
My brother became a diplomat in order to travel around the world.	أصبح أخي دبلوماسياً حتى يسافر حول العالم.
I laughed until I cried.	ضحكت حتى دمعت.
How many days remain until Christmas?	كم يوماً يبقى حتى حلول عيد الميلاد؟
We went to the capital in order to visit the National Museum.	ذهبنا إلى العاصمة حتى نزور المتحف الوطني.
He asked many questions in order to understand the meaning of the text.	سأل أسئلة كثيرة حتى يفهم معنى النص.
The family stayed in Beirut until the end of the war.	بقيتْ العائلة في بيروت حتى نهاية الحرب.
You cannot leave until you have finished your homework.	لا تستطيع الخروج حتى انجزت واجباتك.
90 percent have cast their vote up to now.	٩٠ % يصوّتون حتى الآن.

Arabic–English glossary
قاموس عربي – انجليزي

Although it was mentioned earlier that most Arabic–English dictionaries are organized according to the root letters, this glossary is not. For the sake of easy handling the Arabic words have been sorted alphabetically. The Arabic words are also not fully vocalized, instead only the short vowels necessary for reading have been added. Broken plurals have been included when necessary. They are introduced by the Arabic letter ج. The Roman numbers mark the pattern of the verb. Each verb is listed with its three important forms: the past tense, the present tense and the مصدر.

حرف ا

to smile	اِبتسم - يبتسِم - الابتِسام VIII
son	اِبن ج أبناء
Abu Dhabi	أبو ظبي
white	أبيض - بَيضاء
bus	أتوبيس
furniture	أثاث
to influence	أثَّر - يأثِّر - التأثير II
two, second	اِثنان - الثاني
to answer	أجاب - يجيب - الاجابة IV
to meet, gather	إجتمع - يجتمِع - الاجتِماع VIII
meeting, gathering	إجتِماع
foreign	أجنَبي ج أجانِب
to love	أحبّ - يحِبّ - الحُبّ IV
to occupy	إحتلّ - يحتلّ - الاحتِلال VIII
to be bearable, possible, tolerable	إحتمل - يحتمِل - الاحتِمال VIII

184 Arabic–English glossary

red	أحمَر – حَمراء
to turn red	احمرّ – يحمرّ – الإحمِرار IX
stupid	أحمَق
brother	أخ ج إخوة
sister	أُخت ج أخَوات
test	اِختِبار
to differ	اِختلف – يختلف – الاختِلاف VIII
to take	أخذ – يأخذ – الأخذ I
last, other	آخر
green	أخضر – خَضراء
literature	أدب ج آداب
ear	أُذن ج آذان
to want	أراد – يريد – الإرادة IV
four, fourth	أربعة – الرابِع
to commit (an error)	اِرتكب – يرتكب – الارتِباك VIII
Jordan	الأُرُدن
to send	أرسل – يرسل – الارسال IV
land, soil, ground	أرض ج أراضي
blue	أزرق – زَرقاء
Spain	إسبانيا
week	أُسبوع ج أسابيع
to rent	اِستأجر – يستأجر – الاستِئجار X
professor	أُستاذ ج أساتِذة
to invest	اِستثمر – يستثمر – الاستِثمار X
strategy	الاستراتيجية
to seek help	اِستعان – يستعين – الاستِعانة X
to prepare, to get ready	اِستعدّ – يستعدّ – الاستِعداد X
to resign	اِستقال – يستقيل – الاستِقالة X
to receive, to welcome	اِستقبل – يستقبل – الاستِقبال X
to enjoy	اِستمتع – يستمتع – الاستِمتاع X
to listen	اِستمع – يستمع – الاستِماع VIII
to import	اِستورد – يستورد – الاستِيراد X
to wake (someone)	اِستيقظ – يستيقظ – الاستِيقاظ X

Islam	الاسلام
nuclear weapons	أسلحة نَوَوية
noun, name	إِسم ج أَسماء
black	أسود – سَوداء
to participate	إشترك – يشترك – الاشتِراك VIII
to buy	إشترى – يشتري – الشِراء VIII
to work, to be busy	إشتغل – يشتغل – الاشتِغال VIII
yellow	أصفر – صَفراء
genitive construct	إضافة
to consider	إعتبر – يعتبر – الاعتِبار VIII
to admire, to like	أعجب – يعجب – الإعجاب IV
ordinal numbers	الأعداد التَرتيبية
case endings	إعراب
to give	أعطى – يعطي – العَطاء IV
to inform	أعلن – يعلن – الإعلان IV
blind	أعمى
to close	أغلق – يغلق – الإغلاق IV
song	أُغنية ج أغاني
to set up, to reside	أقام – يقيم – الإقامة IV
residence	إقامة
economy	إقتِصاد
to complete	إكتمل – يكتمل – الاكتِمال VIII
to eat	أكل – يأكل – الأكل I
except	إلا
to meet	إلتقى – يلتقي – الالقاء VIII
who, that (*relative pronoun*)	الذي – التي – الذين
to cancel	أغلى – يلغي – الالغاء IV
to, at	إلى
mother	أُم ج أُمَهات
as . . . is concerned	أمّا ... ف
the Emirates	الإمارات
in front of	أمامَ
imam	إمام

186 *Arabic–English glossary*

test	إمتِحان
woman	إمرَأة ج نِساء
America	أمريكا
yesterday	أمَس
to grab	أمسك – يمسك – الإمساك IV
possibility	إمكانية
security	أمن
admiral	أمير البَحر
that	إنّ
verbal connector	أنْ
that	أنّ
now	الآن
I	أنا
you (*masc.*)	أنتَ
you (*fem.*)	أنتِ
production	إنتاج
to move	إنتقل – ينتقل – الانتِقال VIII
you all	أنتُم
you two	أنتُما
to finish	إنتهى – ينتهي – الانتِهاء VIII
accomplishment	إنجاز ج انجازات
to succeed	أنجَح – ينجح – النَجاح I
to accomplish	أنجَز – ينجز – الانجاز IV
English	إنجليزي
to withdraw, to retreat	إنسحب – ينسحب – الانسِحاب VII
to leave, to withdraw	إنصرف – ينصرف – الانصِراف VII
to meet, to convene	إنعقد – ينعقد – الانعِقاد VII
nose	أنف ج أُنوف
to cut	إنقطع – ينقطع – الانقِطاع VII
the pyramids	الأهرام
more important	أهَمّ
operetta	اوبِريت
Europe	أوروبّا

Arabic–English glossary 187

first	أوّل / أُولى
as well, also	أيضاً
email	إيميل
where?	أين

حرف ب

door, gate	باب ج أبواب
cold	بارِد
to sell	باع - يبيع - البيع I
to find	بحث - يبحث - البَحث I
Bahrain	البَحرين
little lake, pond	بُحَيْرة
innovative	بَديع
orange	بُرتُقال
orange (color)	بُرتقالي
parliament	البَرلَمان
program	بَرنامَج ج بَرامِج
because of	بِسَبَب
card	بِطاقة
hero	بَطل ج أبطال
slowly	بَطيئا
after	بَعدَ أنْ
after that	بَعدَ ذَلِكَ
far, distant	بَعيد
Baghdad	بَغداد
Baklava	بقلاوة
B.A.	بكالوريوس
how much?	بِكَم
to cry	بكي - يبكى - البُكاء I
country, town	بَلَد ج بُلدان
daughter	بِنت ج بَنات
tomato	بَنَدورة
purple	بَنفسَجي
to build	بنى - يبني - البِناء I

188 *Arabic–English glossary*

album	البوم
report	بَيان
house	بَيْت ج بُيوت
Beirut	بيروت
between	بَين
while	بَيْنَما

حرف ت

to exchange	تبادل – يتبادل – التبادُل VI
trade	تِجارة
below, under (*preposition*)	تَحْتَ
civilization	تَحَضُّر
to graduate	تخرّج – يتخرّج – التخرّج V
to specialize	تخصّص – يتخصّص – التخصّص V
to remember	تذكّر – يتذكّر – التذكّر V
education, pedagogy	التَّربية
to translate	ترجم – يترجم – التَّرجَمة I
to leave	ترك – يترك – التَّرك I
nine, ninth	تِسعة – التاسِع
intensification, escalation	تَصعيد
to develop	تطوّر – يتطوّر – التطوّر V
to work together	تعامل – يتعامل – التعامل VI
cooperation	تَعاوُن
tired	تَعبان
to get to know, to meet	تعرّف – يتعرّف – التعرّف V
to learn	تعلّم – يتعلّم – التعلّم V
to be absent	تغيّب – يتغيّب – التغيّب V
apples	تُفاح
to watch	تفرّج – يتفرّج – التفرّج V
to talk	تكلّم – يتكلّم – التكلّم V
to consist of	تكوّن – يتكوّن – التكوّن V
television	تَلِفِزيون
telephone	تَليفون
to be complete	تمّ – يتمّ – التَّمام I

Arabic–English glossary 189

date	تَمَر
to wish	تمنّى - يتمنّى - التمني V
nunation	تَنوين
monotheism	تَوْحيد
Tunisia	تونس

حرف ث

resource, wealth	ثِروة
culture	ثَقافة
three, the third	ثَلاثة ـ الثالث
eight, the eighth	ثَمانية ـ الثامن

حرف ج

to come	جاء - يجيء - المَجيء I
neighbor	جار ج جيران
mosque	جامع ج جوامِع
university	جامِعة
ready	جاهِز
algebra	الجَبر
mountain	جَبَل ج جِبال
grandfather	جَدّ ج أجداد
grandmother	جَدّة
very	جداً
new	جَديد ج جُدُد
root	جَذر ج جُذور
jar	جَرّة
bell	جَرَس
to take place	جرى - يجري - الجَري I
Algeria	الجَزائر
island	جَزيرة ج جُزُر
great, outstanding	جَلّ
group	جَماعة
beauty	جَمالة
masses	جَماهير

190 *Arabic–English glossary*

plural	جَمع
sentence	جُملة
nominal sentence	الجُملة الإسمية
conditional sentence	جُملة الشَرط
descriptive sentence	جُملة الصِفة
verbal sentence	الجُملة الفِعلية
republic	جُمهورية
all	جَميع
beautiful	جَميل
next to	جَنبَ
device, gadget	جِهاز ج أجهِزة
weather	جَوْ
answer	جَواب ج أجوِبة
hungry	جوعان
great, well, good	جَيّد
army	جَيش ج جُيوش

حرف ح

hot	حارّ
to memorize	حافظ – يُحافظ – الحِفظ III
situation, condition	حال ج أحوال
until, even	حَتى
Haji pilgrim	حاجّ ج حُجاج
the Islamic Pilgrimage, Hajj	الحَجّ
event	حَدَث ج أحداث
modern	حَديث
garden	حَديقة ج حَدائق
war	حَرب ج حُروب
letter	حَرف ج حُروف
non-aligned movement	حَرَكة عَدَم الإنحِياز
emphatic letters	حُروف مُفَخّمة
freedom	حُرّية
nice	حَسَن
assassin	حَشاشين

Arabic–English glossary 191

blockade	حِصار
to get, to obtain	حصل – يحصل – الحصول I
to attend	حضر – يحضر – الحُضور I
right, law	حَقّ ج حُقوق
to fulfill, to realize	حقّق – يحقّق – التحقيق II
government	حُكومة
mother-in-law	حَماة

حرف خ

to fear, to be afraid	خاف – يخاف – الخَوْف I
uncle (maternal)	خال ج أخوال
to bake	خبز – يخبِز – الخَبز I
bread	خُبز ج أخباز
expert	خَبير ج خبراء
to leave, to go out	خرج – يخرج – الخُروج I
Khartoum	الخَرطوم
fall, autumn	خَريف
to lose	خسر – يخسر – الخَسارة I
to crackle, to rattle	خَشخَش – يخشخش – الخَشخَشة I
line	خَطّ ج خُطوط
error	خَطأ ج أخطاء
five, the fifth	خَمسة – الخامس
algorithm	الخوارزمي
choice, option	خِيار
fine, well	خَير

حرف د

student, learner	دارِس
always	دائماً
bear	دُبّ
Dubai	دُبي
to enter	دخل – يدخل – الدُخول I
to smoke	دخّن – يدخّن – التدخين II
temperature	دَرَجة الحَرارة

192 *Arabic–English glossary*

to chat	دَردَش – يدردش – الدردشة
to study	درس – يدرس – الدَرس I
study, lesson	دَرس ج دُروس
to invite	دعا – يدعو – الدَعوة I
advocates	دُعاة
notebook	دَفتَر ج دَفاتِر
to knock, to ring	دقّ – يدُقّ – الدقّ I
minute	دَقيقة ج دَقائق
doctor	دُكتور ج دَكاتِرة
doctorate	الدُكتوراه
guide	دَليل
Damascus	دِمشَق
to shed tears	دمع – يدمع – الدَمع I
tears	دُموع
Doha	الدوحة
country, state	دَولة ج دُوَل
democracy	ديموقراطية
diwan	ديوان

حرف ذ

to slaughter, butcher	ذبح – يذبح – الذبح I
smart	ذَكور، ذكي ج أذكياء
that	ذَلِكَ
to go	ذهب – يذهب – الذِهاب I
golden	ذَهَبي

حرف ر

salary, wage	راتِب ج رَواتِب
rest, comfort	راحة
excellent	رائع
Rabat	الرَباط
quarter	رُبع
to return	رجع – يرجع – الرُجوع I

Arabic–English glossary 193

man	رَجُل ج رِجال
to welcome	رحّب - يرحّب - الترحيب II
journey	رِحلة
to respond	ردّ - يردّ - الردّ I
reply	ردّ ج رُدود
letter, message	رِسالة ج رَسائِل
email	الرِسالة الإلكترونية
official	رَسمي
to lift, to raise	رفع - يرفع - الرَفع I
thin, slender	رَفيع
number	رَقم ج أرقام
gray	رَمادي
novel	رِواية
kindergarten	رَوْضة
Riyadh	الرِياض
sport	رِياضة
wind	ريح ج أرياح
president	رَئيس ج رُؤَساء

حرف ز

to visit	زار - يزور - الزِيارة I
customer	زَبون ج زَبائِن
agriculture	الزِراعة
giraffe	زِرافة
to plant, farm	زرع - يزرع - الزرع I
almsgiving	زَكاة
colleague	زَميل ج زُمَلاء
pink	زَهري
marriage	زَواج
husband	زَوْج ج أزواج

194 *Arabic–English glossary*

حرف س

hour, watch	ساعة
to help	ساعد – يساعد – المساعَدة III
to travel	سافر – يسافر – السَفَر III
to ask	سأل – يسأل – السُؤال I
reason	سَبَب ج أسباب
to swim	سبح – يسبح – السِباحة I
seven, the seventh	سَبعة – السابع
way, route	سَبيل ج سُبُل
six, the sixth	سِتّة – السادس
to record, to score	سجّل – يسجّل – التسجيل II
to steal	سرق – يسرِق – السِرقة I
fast, quickly	سَريع
price	سِعر ج أسعار
Saudi Arabia	السعودية
happy	سَعيد
safari	السَفَر
railway	سِكّة حَديدية
inhabitants	سُكّان
sugar	سُكَّر
to live, to reside	سكن – يسكن – السَكن I
vowel marker sukuun	سُكون
knife	سَكينة
weapons	سِلاح ج أسلِحة
safety	السَلامة
turtle	سُلَحفاة
to link	سلْسل – يسلسل – السِلسِلة I
salad	سَلَطة
to greet	سلّم – يسلّم – التَسليم II
sky	سَماء
to allow	سمح – يسمح – السَماح I
to name	سمّى – يسمّي – التسمية II
tooth	سِنّ ج أسنان
year	سَنة ج سَنوات، سِنين

Arabic–English glossary 195

annually	سَنَوياً
to stay up late, to party	سهر – يسهر – السَهر I
easy	سَهل
interrogative, question word	سُؤال ج أسئلة
Sudan	السودان
wall	سور
Syria	سوريا
market	سُوق ج أسواق
Sweden	السويد
car	سَيّارة
policy	سِياسة
political, politician	سِياسي
cigarette	سِيجارة
to rule, to control	سَيطر – يسيطر – السيطرة

حرف ش

guy	شاب ج شَباب
street	شارِع ج شَوارِع
beach	شاطئ
to watch	شاهد – يشاهد – المُشاهَدة III
winter	شِتاء
tree	شَجَرة ج أشجار
person	شَخص ج أشخاص
short vowel shadda	شَدّة
to drink	شرِب – يشرب – الشُرب I
to explain	شرح – يشرح – الشَرح I
company	شَرِكة
popular	شَعبي
hair	شَعر
to feel	شعر – يشعر – الشُعور I
apartment	شَقّة ج شِقَق
sun	شَمس
bag	شَنطة
to witness	شهد – يشهد – الشهود I

196 *Arabic–English glossary*

month	شَهر ج شُهور، أشهر
soup	شوربة
consultation	شورى
thing	شَيء ج أشياء

حرف ص

friend, companion	صاحِب ج أصحاب
morning	صَباح
to wake up	صَحا – يصحو – الصحو I
health	صِحّة
correct, right	صَحيح
friend	صَديق ج أصدِقاء
difficult	صَعب
difficulty	صُعوبة
small	صَغير ج صغار
class, lesson	صَفّ ج صُفوف
adjective	صِفة
prayer	صَلاة
Sanaa	صَنعاء
correct	صَواب
voice	صَوت ج أصوات
to vote	صوّت – يصوّت – التصويت II
picture	صَوْرة ج صُوَر
summer	صَيْف
China	الصين

حرف ض

to laugh	ضحك – يضحك – الضَحِك I
necessary	ضَروري
against	ضِدّ
frog	ضَفدَع
pronouns	ضَمير ج ضَمائر
conscience	ضَمير
guest	ضَيْف ج ضُيوف

Arabic–English glossary   197

حرف ط

floor	طابِق ج طَوابِق
student	طالِب ج طُلّاب
table	طاوِلة
airplane	طائِرة
medicine	الطِبّ
to cook	I طبخ - يطبخ - الطَبخ
nature	طَبيعة
natural	طَبيعي
to raise a question	IV طرح - يطرح - الطَرح
side	طَرَف ج أطراف
way, path, road	طَريق ج طُرُق
food	طَعام
child	طِفل ج أطفال
childhood	طُفولة
weather	طَقس
to demand	I طلب - يطلب - الطَلَب
tomato	طَماطِم
vaccine	طَميم
adobe	الطوبة
tall	طَويل ج طِوال

حرف ظ

injustice	ظُلم
to think	I ظنّ - يظنّ - الظَنّ
noon	ظُهر

حرف ع

to live	I عاش - يعيش - العَيش
capital	عاصِمة ج عَواصِم
well-being	عافية
world	العالَم
high, tall	عالي
year	عام ج أعوام

198 Arabic–English glossary

dialect	عامية
number	عَدَد ج أعداد
lens	عَدَسة
justice	عَدل
Iraq	العِراق
Arabic	عَرَبي
dinner	عَشاء
ten, tenth	عَشَرة – العاشر
member	عُضو ج أعضاء
thirsty	عَطشان
to gather	عقد – يعقِد – العَقد I
relation	عَلاقة
flag	عَلَم ج أعلام
science	عِلم ج عُلوم
scientific	عِلمي
on, at	عَلى
paternal uncle	عَمّ ج أعمام
tall building	عِمارة
Amman	عَمان
Oman	عُمان
to work	عمل – يعمل – العَمل I
to suffer	عاني – يعاني – المعاناة III
at, with (preposition)	عَنَد
when	عَندَما
lute	العَوْد
return	عَوْدة
feast, holiday	عِيد ج أعياد
eye	عَيْن ج عُيون

حرف غ

to leave, to depart	غادر – يغادر – المغادَرة III
expensive	غالي
lunch	غَداء
room	غُرفة ج غُرَف

Arabic–English glossary   199

strange	غَريب
to be angry	غضب - يغضب - الغَضب I
absence	غِياب
un-, non-, il-	غَير
unlikely	غَيْر مُحتَمَل
illegal	غَيْر شَرعي

حرف ف

corrupt	فاسِد
empty	فاغِر
young girl	فَتاة
time period	فَترة
butterfly	فَراشة
person	فَرد ج أفراد
to force	فرض - يفرِض - الفَرض I
team	فِرقة ج فِرَق
France	فرنسا
dress	فُستان ج فَساتين
to fail	فشل - يفشل - الفشل I
Modern Standard Arabic (MSA)	فُصحى
semester, section	فَصل ج فُصول
silver	فِضّي
breakfast	فُطور
verb	فِعل
to do	فعل - يفعل - الفِعل I
to consider, to reflect	فكّر - يفكّر - التَفكير II
Palestine	فِلَسطين
philosophy	فَلسَفة
film	فِلم ج أفلام
art	فَنّ ج فُنون
to understand	فهم - يفهم - الفَهم I
immediately	فَوْراً
in, at (preposition)	في
in reality	في الصَراحة

200 Arabic–English glossary

vitamins	فيتامينات
video	فيديو
physics	الفيزياء
elephant	فيل

حرف ق

to meet	قابل – يقابل – المقابَلة III
(Sultan) Qabus	قابوس
upcoming	قادِم
reader	قارئ
to say	قال – يقول – القَوْل I
dictionary	القاموس
Cairo	القاهِرة
before	قَبلَ أنْ
ugly	قَبيح
ability	قِدرة
Jerusalem	القُدس
old	قَديم ج قُدَماء
decision	قِرار
to decide	قرّر – يقرّر – التقرير II
near relative	قَريب ج أقارِب
village	قَرية ج قُرى
installment	قَسط ج أقساط
department, section	قِسم ج أقسام
story	قِصّة ج قِصَص
castle	قَصر ج قُصور
short	قَصير
to spend (time)	قضى – يقضي – القَضاء I
Qatar	قَطَر
cotton	قُطْن
heart	قَلْب ج قُلوب
to decrease	قلّل – يقلّل – التقليل II
pen	قَلَم ج أقلام
pencil	قَلَم رُصاص

Arabic–English glossary 201

garbage	قُمامة
moon	قَمَر
satellite	قَمَر صِناعي
channel	قَناة
coffee	قَهْوَة
grammar	قَواعِد
force, strength	قُوَّة
strong	قَوي ج أقوياء

حرف ك

nightmare	كابوس
writer, author	كاتِب ج كُتّاب
cup, glass	كأس ج كؤوس
complete	كامِل
to be	كان – يكون – الكَوْن I
kebab	كَباب
big, old	كَبير ج كِبار
book	كِتاب ج كُتُب
to write	كتب – يكتب – الكِتابة I
cafeteria	كافيتريا
many	كَثير
alcohol	الكحول
liar	كَذوب
generosity	كَرامة
ball	كُرة
basketball	كُرة السَلة
football	كُرة القَدَم
chair	كُرسي ج كَراسي
generous	كَريم ج كِرام
to gain	كسب – يكسب – الكسب I
dog	كَلب ج كِلاب
word	كَلِمة
college	كُلِّية
how many?	كَم

202 Arabic–English glossary

treasure	كَنز ج كُنوز
Kuwait	الكُوَيْت
how?	كَيفَ
chemistry	الكيمياء

حرف ل

for (*preposition*)	لِ
refugee	لاجئ ج ون
player	لاعِب ج ون
because	لأنَّ
to wear	لبِس – يلبس – اللُبس I
Lebanon	لُبْنان
at, with	لَدى
yummy	لَذيذ
friendly, nice	لَطيف ج لُطَفاء
to play	لعِب – يلعب – اللَعِب I
language	لُغة
stork	لَقلَق
to meet	لقِيَ – يلقى – اللقاء I
but	لكِن
in order to	لِكَي
negator for past tense	لم
when	لما
why?	لِماذا
negator for future tense	لَن
London	لُندُن
God	الله
pearl	لؤلؤ
Libya	ليبيا
negator for "to be" and "to have"	لَيسَ
night	لَيلة ج لَيالٍ
lemon	لَيمون

Arabic–English glossary 203

حرف م

what?	ما
except	ما عَدا
water	ماء
what? (*verbal question*)	ماذا
effective, influential	مُؤَثِّر
past tense	الماضي
Germany	ألمانيا
game, match	مُباراة ج مُباريات
principle	مَبدأ ج مَبادئ
congratulations!	مَبروك
early	مُبَكِّر
building	مَبنى ج مَباني
late	مُتَأَخِّر
museum	مَتحَف ج مَتاحِف
graduate	مُتَخَرِّج ج ون
translator	مُتَرجِم ج ون
demands, requirements	مُتَطَلَّبات
accused, defendant	مُتَّهَم
expected	مُتَوَقَّع
saying, proverb	مَثَل ج أمثال
like (*comparison*)	مِثلَ
snowy	مُثلِج
dual	المُثنى
diligent	مُجتَهِد
genitive	المجرور
verbal mode with sukuun	المجزوم
council, assembly	مَجلِس
conversation	مُحادَثة
lecture	مُحاضَرة
popular, favorite, beloved	مَحبوب
station	مَحَطّة
store	مَحَلّ

204 *Arabic–English glossary*

Muhammad	مُحَمَّد
bakery	مَخْبَز
chosen	مُخْتار
magazine	مَخْزَن ج مَخازِن
camp	مُخَيَّم
time period	مُدّة
entry	مَدخَل
teacher	مُدَرِّس ج ون
school	مَدرَسة ج مَدارِس
director	مُدير ج مُدَراء
city	مَدينة ج مُدُن
Medina	المَدينة المُنَوَّرة
masculine	مُذَكَّر
broadcaster	مُذيعة
correspondent	مُراسِل
verbal mode with Damma	المرفوع
center	مَرْكَز ج مراكِز
sick, ill	مَريض ج مَرضى
disturbing, bothering	مُزعِج
evening	مَساء
responsible, in charge	مَسؤول ج ون
swimming pool	مَسبَح ج مَسابِح
used	مُستَعمَل
future tense	المُستَقبَل
mosque	مَسجِد ج مَساجِد
theater	مَسرَح ج مَسارِح
Masqat	مَسقَط
Muslim	مُسلِم ج ون
participant	مُشارِك ج ون
project	مَشروع ج مَشاريع
busy	مَشغول
problem	مُشكِلة ج مَشاكِل
sunny	مُشمِس

Arabic–English glossary 205

famous	مَشْهور
grilled	مَشوي
to walk	مشى - يَمشي - المَشي I
verbal noun	المَصدَر
Egypt	مصر
prayer hall	مُصَلّى
worshiper	مُصَلّي
factory	مَصنَع ج مَصانِع
present tense	المُضارِع
airport	مَطار
singer	مُطرِب ج ون
restaurant	مَطعَم ج مَطاعِم
absolutely	مُطلَقاً
wanted, desired	مَطلوب
volunteer	مُطَوِّع ج ون
demonstration	مُظاهَرة
oppressed	مَظلوم
agreement	مُعاهَدة
temple	مَعبَد ج مَعابِد
definite	المُعرّف
known	مَعروف
most	مُعظَم
teacher	مُعَلِّم ج ون
institute	مَعهَد ج مَعاهِد
assistant	مُعيد ج ون
Morocco	المَغرِب
closed	مُغلَق
key	مِفتاح ج مَفاتيح
Mufti	مُفتي
singular	مُفرَد
words	مُفرَدات
favorite	مُفَضَّل
thinker, intellectual	مُفَكِّر ج ون

206 *Arabic–English glossary*

understood	مَفهوم
useful	مُفيد
article, paper	مَقالة
seat, place, residence	مَقَرّ
seat	مَقعَد ج مَقاعِد
café	مَقهى – مَقاهي
Mecca	مَكّة المُكَرّمة
place	مَكان ج أماكِن
office	مَكتَب ج مَكاتِب
library	مَكتَبة
vacuum cleaner	مَكنَسة كَهرَبائية
butchery	مَلحَمة
summary	مُلخّص
king	مَلِك ج مُلوك
colorful	مُلوّن
million	مليون
exciting	مُمتِع
rainy	مُمطِر
boring	مُمِلّ
who?	مَن
from (*preposition*)	مِن
in order to, because	من أجل
from where?	مِن أين
appropriate	مُناسِب
team	مُنتَخَب
middle (*time*), mid-	مُنتَصَف
scholarship	مِنحة ج مِنَح
since, ago	مُنذُ
house, settlement	مَنزِل ج مَنازِل
verbal mode with fatHa	المَنصوب
area, region	مِنطَقة ج مَناطِق
non-profit organization	مُنَظّمة غَيْر رِبحية
to forbid, to prevent	منع – يَمنع – المَنع I

Arabic–English glossary 207

indefinite	المُنَكَّر
method	مِنهَج ج مَناهِج
festival	مَهَرَجان
important	مُهِمّ
agreed, OK	مُوافِق
conference	مؤتَمَر
present	مَوجود
bananas	مُوز
organization, institution	مُؤَسَّسة
season	مَوسِم ج مَواسِم
employee	مُوَظَّف ج ون
position, location	مَوقِع ج مَواقِع
feminine	مُؤَنَّث

حرف ن

club	نادي ج أندية
to discuss	ناقش – يناقِش – المُناقَشة III
to sleep	نام – ينام – النَوْم I
representative, deputy	نائب ج نُوّاب
we	نَحْنُ
to descend, to come down	نزل – ينزِل – النُزول I
to forget	نسي – ينسى – النِسيان I
active	نَشيط
to pronounce	نطق – ينطُق – النُطق I
pronunciation	النُطق
to view, to look at	نظر – ينظُر – النَظر I
counterpart	نَظير ج نُظَراء
clean	نَظيف
same, soul	نَفس ج نُفوس، أنفُس
negation	النَفي
point	نُقطة ج نِقاط، نُقَط
end	نِهاية

208 *Arabic–English glossary*

light	نور
type, kind	نَوْع ج أنواع
sleep	نَوْم
to intend	نَوَى – ينوي – النِّيّة I

حرف ه

goal, aim	هَدَف ج أهداف
this	هذا، هذه
escape, flight	هُروب
they	هُم
they two	هُما
they (*fem.*)	هُنّ
here	هُنا
there	هُناك
engineering	هَندَسة
Red Indians	الهُنود الحُمُر
he	هو
hobby	هِواية
those	هَؤُلاء
she	هِيَ

حرف و

one	واحِد
wise, spacious	واسِع
Washington	واشنطن
to say goodbye	ودَّع – يودّع – التَوديع II
rose	وَردة
paper	وَرَقة ج أوراق
ministry	وِزارة
pattern	وَزن ج أوزان
minister	وَزير ج وُزَراء
pillow	وِسادة
dirty	وَسِخ
handsome	وَسيم

Arabic–English glossary 209

to arrive	وصل - يصل - الوُصول I
to put	وضع - يضع - الوَضع I
situation	وَضع ج أوضاع
ablution	وُضوء
homeland	وَطَن ج أوطان
job	وَظيفة ج وَظائف
to provide	وفّر - يوفّر - التَوفير II
time	وَقت ج أوقات
to take place	وقع - يقع - الوُقوع I
to stop	وقف - يقف - الوُقوف I
been born	وُلِدَ
boy	وَلَد ج أولاد

حرف ي

Japan	اليابان
to commit errors	خطى - يُخطئ - الخطأ I
hand	يَد ج أيْدي
Yemen	اليَمَن
day	يَوْم ج أيام
Sunday	يَوْم الأحَد

Bibliography

Alhawary, Mohammad T.: *Arabic Second Language Acquisition of Morphosyntax*, Yale University, 2009.

Al-Wahy, Ahmed Seddik: "Idiomatic False Friends in English and Modern Standard Arabic." In: *Babel* 55: 2 (2009), 101–123.

Hans Wehr: *Arabic–English Dictionary: The Hans Wehr Dictionary of Modern Written Arabic*. Ed. by J. Milton Cowan, Spoken Language Services, 1994.

Palfreyman, D. and M. Al Khalil: "A Funky Language for Teenzz to Use: Representing Gulf Arabic in Instant Messaging". In: *Journal of Computer-Mediated Communication*, vol. 9, issue 1 (November 2003).

Rammuny, Raji: "Statistical Study of Errors Made by American Students in Written Arabic." In: *Al-Arabiyya*, vol. 9 (1976), 74–94.

Salib, Galila Gabriel: *A Study of Common Writing Mistakes by Advanced Learners of Arabic*, American University of Cairo, 1988.

Schulz, Eckehard with Sebastian Maisel: *Al-Arabiya al-Mu'asira – Modern Standard Arabic: Textbook Integrating Main Arabic Dialects*. Edition Hamouda, Leipzig, 2013.

Index and glossary of grammatical terms

The numbers refer to the page numbers in the book. Bold numbers indicate the main information about the grammatical item.

English	عربي
accent, ix	لَهَجة
accusative, 47, **50**, **71–74**	المنصوب
active voice, **93**	صِيغة المَعلوم
adjective, 31–32, 40, 45, 53, **56–62**, 68, 113, 118, 132, 139	صِفة
adverb, 23, 50, 71, **131–132**, 140	ظَرف
alphabet, 2, **14–17**, 26–27, 37	أبجَدية
broken plural, 23, **41–43**, 73–74	الجَمع المكسّر أو جَمع التكسير
cardinal numbers, **113–117**, 120	العَدَد الأساسي
case endings, declension, **66–76**	إعراب
circumstantial clause, 72, **109–110**	جُملة الحال
comparative/superlative, **59–61**	أفعَل
conditional sentence, **104–105**	جُملة الشَرط
culture, 67, 127	ثَقافة
definite, 7, 20, 23, 40–41, 57, 50, 52, 105–106, 118, 136	المُعَرَّف
descriptive sentence, **105–107**	جُملة الصِفة
dialect, 4, **27–28**, 67, 129	عامية
dictionary, 33–34, **37**, 81	القاموس
dual, **41–42**, 74, 85, 106, 113–115	المثنّى
emphatic sounds, 2, **6**	الحُروف المفخّمة
exception clause, **108–109**	جُملة الإستِثناء

212 Index and glossary of grammatical terms

feminine, 42, **45–48**, 57, 63, 114–116, 118–119 — مُؤنَّث

future tense, **79–81**, 90 — المُستَقبَل

genitive, **70–74** — المجرور

genitive construct, 11, 23, **51–53**, 59, 64, 70, 135, 137 — إضافة

grammar, ii, ix — قواعِد

imperative, **89–90** — الأمر

indefinite, 23, 40–41, **47–48**, 50, 68, 97, 105, 113–116, 136 — المنكَّر

interrogative, question, 75, 102–103, **111**, 123–124 — السُؤال

irregular verb, s55, **83–85** — الفِعل الشاذ

letter, **2–9**, **14–15**, 17–18, **20–24**, 26–27, 33–34, 78, 81, 83–85 — حَرَف ج حُروف

masculine, 23, **41–42**, 45–47, 58, 63, 78, 114–116, 118–119 — مُذَكَّر

Modern Standard Arabic (MSA), 4, 27, 53, **67**, 88, 90, 96, 129 — فُصحى

moon letters, **7–8**, **23** — الحُروف القَمَرية

negation, **90–93** — النَفي

nisba – Adjective, 20, **58–60** — النِسبة

nominal sentence, 56, 90, **96–99**, 134 — الجُملة الإسمية

nominative, 47, 50, **69–70**, 72–74 — المرفوع

noun, 23–24, 33, 39, **40–53**, 56–63, 68, 72, 74, 82, 96–99, 105–108, 113–119, 135–139 — إِسم

number, 24–25, 28, **112–125** — عَدَد ج أعداد

nunation, **47–50**, 68–69 — تَنوين

object, 68, 70–71, 75, **86–89**, 96 — النَصَب

object in a verbal sentence, **96**, 98–100 — المَفعول بِه

object pronoun, 22, **86–89** — ضِمير النَصَب

ordinal numbers, **118–120** — الأعداد التَرتيبية

participle: active and passive, **53–56**, 132 — إِسم فاعِل وإِسم مَفعول

passive voice, 81, **93** — صيغة المجهول

past tense, 33, **78**, 85, 87, 90–91, 104, 140 — الماضي

pattern, **30–34**, 42, 51, 54–55, 58–62, 81–82, 89, 115, 118 — وَزن ج أوزان

personal pronoun, **78**, 85–86 — ضَمير شَخصي

plural, **41–45**, 50–51, 57, 61, **72–74**, 78, 89, 106, 114, 116, 136–137 — الجمع

possessive pronoun, 20, **63**, 86 — ضَمير الملكية

predicate in nominal sentence, 69, **96–97** — الخَبر

prefix, 33, **78–79**, 85, 139 — سابِقة

Index and glossary of grammatical terms   213

preposition, 52–53, 55, **70–71**, 91, 111, 119, 131–132	حَرَف جَرّ
present tense, 33, **79–80**, 85, 88–91, 140	المضارع
pronouns, **63–64**, **78**, **86–87**, 106	ضَمائر
pronunciation, 2, **4–9**, 11, 41, 63, 68	النُطْق
relative sentence, **105–107**	جُملة الصِلة
root, **30–33**, **37**, 48, 78, 81, 83–85, 131	جَذر ج جُذور
sentence, 8, 26, 75, 90, **96–112**, 131–134	جُملة
singular, 33, **41–46**, 50, 63, 73, 83–84, 98–99, 114–116, 123	مُفرَد
sound plural, 41–43, 58, **72**	الجَمع السالِم
stress, **10–11**	تَشديد
subject in nominal sentence, **96–97**	المبتدأ
subject in verbal sentence, **98–100**	الفاعِل
suffix, 10, 30, 32–34, 41, 47, 78–79, 118, 136	لاحقة
sun letters, **7–8**, **23**	الحُروف الشَمسية
verb, 22, 33–34, 53–55, **77–94**, 96–100, 134	فِعل
verb conjugation, **78–79**, 83–84, 89	تَصريف الفِعل
verbal mode with Damma, **88–90**	المرفوع
verbal mode with fatHa, **88–90**	المنصوب
verbal mode with kasra, **88–90**	المجزوم
verbal mode with sukuun, **88–90**	المَجزوم
verbal noun, **82–84**, 88, 93	المصدر
verbal sentence, **96–100**, 131, 134	الجُملة الفِعلية

eBooks
from Taylor & Francis
Helping you to choose the right eBooks for your Library

Add to your library's digital collection today with Taylor & Francis eBooks. We have over 50,000 eBooks in the Humanities, Social Sciences, Behavioural Sciences, Built Environment and Law, from leading imprints, including Routledge, Focal Press and Psychology Press.

Choose from a range of subject packages or create your own!

Benefits for you
- Free MARC records
- COUNTER-compliant usage statistics
- Flexible purchase and pricing options
- 70% approx of our eBooks are now DRM-free.

Benefits for your user
- Off-site, anytime access via Athens or referring URL
- Print or copy pages or chapters
- Full content search
- Bookmark, highlight and annotate text
- Access to thousands of pages of quality research at the click of a button.

Free Trials Available

We offer free trials to qualifying academic, corporate and government customers.

eCollections
Choose from 20 different subject eCollections, including:
- Asian Studies
- Economics
- Health Studies
- Law
- Middle East Studies

eFocus
We have 16 cutting-edge interdisciplinary collections, including:
- Development Studies
- The Environment
- Islam
- Korea
- Urban Studies

For more information, pricing enquiries or to order a free trial, please contact your local sales team:

UK/Rest of World: **online.sales@tandf.co.uk**
USA/Canada/Latin America: **e-reference@taylorandfrancis.com**
East/Southeast Asia: **martin.jack@tandf.com.sg**
India: **journalsales@tandfindia.com**

www.tandfebooks.com